HEISEI SHIATSU

平静指圧

Deep shiatsu and the no-pain principle

Fernando Cabo

ISBN 978-1-7395296-0-4

Notes:

1) All names in the case histories presented in this book have been changed to keep the identity of patients and/or students confidential.

2) All points on meridians are given Japanese pronunciation in brackets rather than the Chinese one. The localisation of points are the same in both countries and languages, but a few of the ideograms are different. The pronunciation is different in each language.

Dedicated to Neil and Isaac.

Neil, without the opportunities you gave me, this book would be but a distant dream.

Isaac, all those conversations, in which you always made me laugh, were the spark for many of the ideas in this book. As you once said, you are my muse.

The last chapter is dedicated to all those who,
after reading it, may think I was writing about them.
I was

Contents:

Foreword 11

Prologue 11

Introduction 15

Chapter 1

Shiatsu: different styles, common basics

What is shiatsu? 21
The basics of shiatsu 22
The different styles 24
Confusion in the literature 25
Empathy 26

Chapter 2

Would you believe it?

Deep is not the same as hard or strong

Dispelling the myth 29
The physics of shiatsu 30
Deep and hard (or strong) are different, and so are soft
and shallow 32
Is Heisei Shiatsu a type of medical shiatsu? 33
Case history: what you see is not what you get 33

Chapter 3

What beginners do

Better the whole weight than half the weight 35
Our intention affects movement 36
Your height matters and other tips 38
Case history: how my teaching changed 39

Chapter 4

Ways of pressing: our body as a tool

The thumb 44
The thumbs and fingers in Heisei Shiatsu 48
The palms of the hands 50
Elbows and knees 51
Characteristics of pressure 51
Case history: when I take criticism of my shiatsu from other shiatsu therapists as high praise 52

Chapter 5

I can repeat it a thousand times...

...but I cannot say it clearer

I cannot say it clearer 55
The invisible perception 59
Case history: excruciating back pain at the hospital 61

Chapter 6

The importance of touch:

science, shiatsu and the quest for quality

Attitudes towards science 63
Touch and science 68
The quest for quality 70

Chapter 7

Relax,

your tension affects your treatment

Posture and pressure are related 73
Pressure intensity matters 74
The arms change position, I don't 75
Intention revisited 76
Case history: when students find it hard to relax 77
Case history: toe rotations 77

Chapter 8

Speed & rhythm

Entering and exiting 80
Rhythm and speed 82
Adapt your shiatsu to the person 83
Static holds 84
Case history: speed change to reduce pain in difficult
situations 85

Chapter 9

The no-pain principle

The no-pain principle 86
How to reduce intensity of pressure 88
Case history: at the hospital 89
Case history: a private client 90
Speed revisited 91
When is it difficult to apply the no-pain principle? 91
初心 Beginner's mind 92

Chapter 10

Shiatsu and the relaxation response

Stress 95
The relaxation response 96
Why depth of pressure matters: a physiological point of
view 97
Case history: anxiety, or speed revisited again 98
Case history: shiatsu and relaxation 99
Heisei Shiatsu as movement meditation: a case history
.... 100

Chapter 11

Abdominal shiatsu (腹指圧)

The benefits 102
The no-pain principle revisited: our speed once more
.... 103
Abdominal shiatsu to aid digestion 104
Natural versus forced breathing 108

Chapter 12

Improvement of health conditions is not all or nothing, it can be gradual

Case history: when you don't give a therapy a chance
.... 112
Treating musculoskeletal problems 113
Treatment 1: low back pain 113
Treatment 2: neck stiffness 115

Chapter 13

Working on the massage table is the same. How to adapt shiatsu to any situation

Shiatsu in Japan: practicality 118
Gravity revisited 121
Case history: treating a patient in a wheelchair 122

Chapter 14

Thank God for small mercies

One of my current roles 124

The strange case of shiatsu and osteoporosis
.... 126

Case history: I thought you were going to rip me apart
.... 127

Chapter 15

Have I finally discovered why?

A mystifying shiatsu story 129

How and why some shiatsu therapists' pressure is painful
.... 138

Case history: working with the no-pain principle in difficult
circumstances 140

Two case histories: inconveniencing the patients less than
other therapists 141

Epilogue 144

References & Bibliography 147

Index 152

Foreword

I met Fernando in early January 2023 at Bart's Hospital in London where I was an inpatient being treated for cancer.

He gave me a few shiatsu treatments while I was lying on the reclining sofa. Although I suffer from pain all over my body, the massage itself was painless, and it helped reduce my pain. I should add that his treatments are very relaxing and I always fall asleep. Amazingly, as I have said before, there is pain all over my body, but Fernando can spot the right places to press to make me feel relaxed.

Luciane Monteiro-Vieira
London, March 2023

Prologue

I have been working as a shiatsu therapist with cancer patients in a hospital in London since 2015. The hospital was the setting where I collected data for my Master's dissertation which was entitled 'Shiatsu Massage as an Adjunct to the Pharmacological Management of Cancer Pain'. What I did was to give shiatsu treatments to patients who complained of any type of pain. In some cases, the pain preceded the cancer diagnosis and had become chronic. Apart from the positive effects the treatment had helping with their pain in almost all cases, the patients invariably commented on how relaxed they felt after the treatments, usually saying they felt like sleeping. Not all patients I treat or I have treated suffer from pain, but, according to them, they enjoy the shiatsu sessions, and they find them very relaxing.

We are talking here about inpatients, patients who are hospitalised, who lie in their beds and whom the nurses, doctors, physiotherapists, occupational therapists and others need to visit regularly. This makes the work of the integrative therapists more unsystematic and haphazard.

You never know when it is the right time to pay the patients a visit to treat them, and quite a few times we need to either go back several times to see if they are free, or even interrupt our treatments because the doctors need to talk to the patient, or the patient needs to go for a scan or for another procedure.

One day, I was treating one patient, when a doctor came in to see the patient, so I left the room. I was outside writing my notes for about two minutes, when the same doctor tapped me on my shoulder and said that the patient had basically cut him short and asked him to tell me to go back and continue the treatment. The doctor appeared to be mildly amused and was smiling while asking me to go back to finish my massage.

Although shiatsu is very beneficial, it is not a panacea and I don't consider myself a magician or someone who comes up with miracle cures. I find it funny to hear students sometimes ask about particular points on the body and their properties. What is the point for back pain? What is the point for constipation? They want to get immediate results, and they want results 100% of the time, which means they want to be magicians, not shiatsu therapists. Whenever they ask these type of questions, I tell them the anecdote of what happened to me in the first place I started working with shiatsu. I was above a hairdresser's whose receptionist took the appointments for shiatsu. All of them, the receptionist and the hairdressers, were women, and many times I chatted with them when we were not busy. I don't remember if it was the first or second day I was there when they asked me: what is the point I have to press to make my boss give me a salary increase? I laughed out loud, and was happy to discover their sense of humour. Remember! If you discover that point, let us know. Many of us would like to try!

A point may *help* with certain conditions, and I give a couple of examples in the treatments for back pain and neck stiffness in the book, but I don't think that pressing one point is the solution to any health condition.

As you will discover in this book, first, I consider the body as a whole and shiatsu to be a holistic therapy, and second, in my experience, it is much more important *how* you press, the *quality* of your pressure, than pressing specific points. Good pressure has a more profound effect as you will discover in the pages of this book.

Acquiring the enjoyable, soft - but at the same time deep - pressure I am espousing in this book, and which I use in my practice, cannot be done overnight. It is a process, a journey, and my beginnings in this journey were not particularly auspicious.

When I first started learning shiatsu my pressure was hard and most of the "guinea pigs" – or volunteers if you prefer - I worked on, said it was sometimes painful, probably about 50% of the time, although they also said they felt very relaxed at the end. Even in those days I must have been doing something right, because they all came back for my "treatments". It was only after many hours of practice and my constant prodding to get a reply to the question on whether my pressure was "good" or "bad", painful or painless, deep or superficial, that little by little my pressure became what it is today. To a certain extent, I believe that my pressure being so hard in those days was a blessing.

It made me think a lot about it and it forced me somehow to pay more attention to it than I would otherwise have. It also gave me the opportunity to learn from my mistakes and be able to transmit this knowledge to other people and show them how to make their pressure soft and deep. When learning shiatsu, I was so passionate that I practised a lot, at every opportunity, and I am happy to say that by the time I graduated, all of my colleagues said what a nice pressure I had acquired.

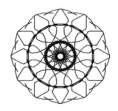

Introduction

I began working professionally with shiatsu in 2001 and teaching it in 2007. When teaching short introductory courses, some of the participants expressed how they always wanted either me or my assistants to demonstrate on them because our pressure was much nicer than the pressure applied by the beginners.

As many of my patients had also told me how they liked my pressure, I simply assumed it was a question of beginner versus experienced practitioner.

My perception changed one day, when I was teaching how to treat menstrual disorders to a group of advanced students. One of the students explained that she always suffered from headaches when she had her period which she did on that day. The students and I decided to work on the Spleen Meridian. I was demonstrating, when the student said the treatment was relieving her headache. As is my custom, I let one of the students continue, when our subject said it was not helping. Asked why, she replied, because you, the teacher, were pressing in a different way.

At that moment, I realised that quality of pressure is probably more important than anything else in shiatsu, so my way of teaching changed. I began checking students' pressure much more often and gave them instructions for improving it. I realised that some of the students' pressure was too hard, and yet, others' was not deep enough.

Hard pressure does not allow the receiver to relax and can be painful, while too light or superficial pressure is felt as if it does not reach, as if it does not have a profound effect.

One of my students described it as if somebody offered you a sweet and, when you are going to put it in your mouth, they suddenly take it away from you.

Throughout the years my students and my patients have been my teachers, and continue to be, for one never stops learning.

Thanks to their comments and their replies to my endless questions we were able to see that the most effective, soothing and enjoyable pressure is when it is deep and painless. Deep, but not strong, hard or pointy.

I know that many therapists in the field of manual therapy would find this contradictory. For them, deeper means harder or stronger. It has taken me many hours of talking and demonstrating to show that this is not the case in our type of shiatsu.

Of course, a good therapist knows how to adapt pressure to the person, and even to the area they are working on. To achieve this deep, painless pressure takes time and patience as well as awareness of one's way of giving shiatsu. But for both the giver and the receiver, it is worth the effort.

Throughout my professional career I have tried many people's shiatsu from many different schools. Some of them had an incredibly good pressure, others were more mediocre. In one instance, the teachers' pressure was of very high quality, but this was not the case for the advanced students. I never said anything of course, but I was convinced that the teachers were not transmitting their knowledge on this very important aspect of shiatsu.

Other shiatsu styles or schools may give more importance to exact points to press, or to diagnosis, or to following a routine and you can find many books with explanations about the details of meridians and points and diagnosis in shiatsu, but I believe this is the first book written about quality of pressure. Although there is merit in teaching all of those approaches, and I teach these aspects of shiatsu too, I believe that without good quality pressure their effectiveness is much reduced.

Over the years, I have introduced quite a few other changes, always adapting shiatsu so that it is easier to give for anyone irrespective of their height and build, and more effective for the conditions patients come to us for help. I call this style Heisei Shiatsu. The name Heisei was chosen by me and some of my students when we were discussing several possibilities. It means serene or calm in Japanese.

In the book I have used technical terms and scientific explanations – which in in any case are mostly hypotheses – sparingly. The basic terminology for those who want to delve deeper can be found in its pages. There are many websites and books that they can refer to.

The last chapter of the book asks why some shiatsu therapists in the UK, where I am based, refuse to introduce shiatsu in hospitals where aromatherapy, reflexology and reiki are offered, (sometimes other therapies are offered too, depending on NHS trust[1], but the number of hospitals that offer shiatsu is miniscule).

Based on my personal experiences, I believe that, after the many, many rejections I have received when applying for voluntary work, and the "reasons" I have heard, I now know why this is the case, which is directly related to their lack of understanding of what good quality pressure in shiatsu is.

---

[1] In the UK, an NHS Trust is in charge of public healthcare in a local area, which includes the public hospitals in that area.

指圧の心は母心、押せば命の泉湧く

The heart of shiatsu is like maternal love.
Pressing on the body makes the wellspring of life flow
Tokujiro Namikoshi

Above all else, guard your heart,
for it is the wellspring of life.
Proverbs 4:23

初心忘るべからず

Never forget the beginner's mind
Zeami Motokiyo

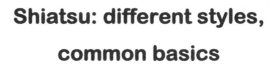

Chapter 1

Shiatsu: different styles, common basics

What is shiatsu?

When I wanted to begin doing research in shiatsu, I was surprised by several things. One, by the very few papers written on the subject, two, by the fact that they seemed to need, in order to support their thesis, research papers based on complete different modalities of bodywork – mostly acupressure – and third and most curious, how in those papers shiatsu was either not defined, or the definitions I encountered referred to one particular style of shiatsu, as if all styles had the same theoretical and practical characteristics. This is why I decided to produce a research paper that gave a definition that could encompass all the styles.

'Shiatsu is a manual therapy applied by leaning forward in a relaxed manner with the weight of one's body to an optimum point, and the correct use of fingers, palms, etc., in order to apply sustained, stationary pressure on different parts of the body for the purpose of correcting the imbalances of the body, and for maintaining and promoting health. It is a holistic therapy that aims to treat most of the body in each session'

Of course, the definition my colleagues and I came up with doesn't encapsulate all aspects of shiatsu, but I believe it is valid as a basic definition.

I have heard some criticisms of this definition. The most interesting one, in my opinion, is that it didn't explain the fact that shiatsu is done through clothing and does not use cream or oils. However, I believe it encapsulates some aspects of what shiatsu is which the official definition of shiatsu in Japan has left out.

The official definition of shiatsu in Japan is: 'Shiatsu is a manual treatment that uses the fingers and the palm of one's hands to apply pressure to particular sections on the surface of the body for the purpose of correcting the imbalances of the body and for maintaining and promoting health. It is also a method contributing to the healing of specific illnesses'.

I have shown our definition to quite a few shiatsu therapists who have not trained with me, and they have all said that it pretty much explains what we do as shiatsu therapists. It is also true that the aim of treating most of the body in each session does not translate into every session in real life, since there might be time, space or other limitations.

The basics of shiatsu

There is something that seems to be unique to shiatsu and Thai massage. Both these techniques seem to be the only ones that work exclusively with the weight of the body. One's own strength does not come into play when giving shiatsu. The use of the relaxed weight of the body to apply pressure is, in my opinion, the most important common thread that unites all styles of shiatsu. Other bodywork therapies also talk about using the weight of the body, but as anyone who has observed how they work, they either don't use the *whole* weight of the body, or they use a mixture of the weight of the body and the strength of the arms.

Seen from the outside, from the point of view of a shiatsu therapist, these other therapies seem to stop the movement of the body half way, to not let go completely with the whole weight and therefore use – at least in part – the strength of their arms.

This is most clearly seen in the movement of the hips. In shiatsu, the hips go all the way with the movement of the shoulders and the torso, because the person is using their whole weight. Although it might sound counterintuitive, going all the way with the *relaxed* weight of one's body makes the pressure softer, more soothing and enjoyable, but still deep at the same time.

Shiatsu, as is well known, is composed of two Japanese ideograms (called kanjis in Japanese), shi 指, which means finger and atsu 圧, which means pressure. I do not think I am the first, nor will I be the last, to point out that the term 'shiatsu' can create the false impression that something heavy and hard, 'pressure', is applied by the shiatsu therapist on the surface of the body. 'Pressure', as the word is usually understood in English, sounds like a hard thing, as if a weight was stopping us from moving or weighing us down. It is only called 'pressure' because it is static as opposed to the circling/rubbing of Swedish Massage or Tui Na, but it can be – and it is in most cases – felt as something truly pleasant as well as deeply relaxing.

Incidentally, when I have asked Japanese people in London who have never received shiatsu what they think about shiatsu, they say the same thing, that they believe it is hard because of the word "pressure".

Curiously, I have personally given shiatsu to quite a few people who didn't enjoy it because it *didn't* cause any pain. For some strange reason I cannot comprehend, they believe that if there is no pain, it is not effective. This is one of the aspects of Heisei Shiatsu that distinguishes it from most styles of Thai Massage and from the way some shiatsu practitioners work.

We believe pressure should be painless, pressure should be enjoyable, and it should be effective. The no-pain principle is one of the basic tenets of Heisei Shiatsu.

The different styles

Nowadays there are quite a few shiatsu styles and many of them have evolved outside Japan although they are in many cases associated with famous names from Japanese masters who developed modern shiatsu in the 20th century. A survey carried out in French-speaking countries identified 26 different styles although 4 of those had no practitioners[2]. By contrast, in the English-speaking world very few styles are mentioned[3]. The best-known pioneers are Shitsuzo Masunaga and Tokujiro Namikoshi, two very influential persons in the world of shiatsu although there are many others[4]. Their respective styles are called Keiraku Shiatsu (Keiraku 経絡 (けいらく) means meridian in Japanese) and Namikoshi Shiatsu. How closely the styles practised nowadays reflect the way these and other pioneers worked, and what has been changed, would be an interesting research project, but beyond the scope of this book[5].

Speaking exclusively from personal observation of how practitioners of other styles work, I do not see huge differences in the practical application of treatments.

There are *some* differences, but in my opinion, not enough to consider all styles anything but shiatsu, at least from the point of view of our definition.

---

[2] https://www.ryohoshiatsu.com/fr/sondage-enquete-de-styles/
[3] The (UK) Shiatsu Society only mentions 8:
https://www.shiatsusociety.org/styles-of-shiatsu
[4] https://www.shiatsu-france.com/article-maitres-du-shiatsu.html
[5] At the time of writing, there is a Facebook group that is researching the history of shiatsu with some of those involved being fluent in Japanese.

Some of the particularities of each style are purely theoretical, on how to diagnose or on which exact points and/or lines to press, some more practical. This book does not delve into the theoretical aspects of any shiatsu style, which can be read in many books and websites. This book is almost exclusively about the more practical aspects of how Heisei Shiatsu was developed without separating from the common basic aspects, which are the movement of the body and the characteristics of pressure, something all styles of shiatsu appear to agree on and follow. These two aspects are explained and interpreted from our point of view in chapters 3 and 4 respectively.

Confusion in the literature

There seems to be some confusion of what shiatsu is compared to other East Asian modalities of bodywork. Although it seems beyond dispute that shiatsu was mostly derived from Anma, the traditional Japanese bodywork technique, it underwent a profound change. In my opinion, the revolution that shiatsu made was that it adopted only one technique from the East Asian bodywork practices from which it is derived, and, I believe, it improved that technique by changing the way it was applied.

This technique is the application of *stationary* pressure. In shiatsu, the arms and the hands are considered as levers through which to transmit the pressure that comes from one's own weight.

Practitioners do nothing with the arms and hands except position them in different ways to change the intensity and the quality of the pressure applied. By contrast, Anma and Tui Na also apply circling or dynamic pressure.

This doesn't mean that one is not allowed to use those other techniques in a shiatsu session or that nobody is permitted to develop a style using as many techniques as they wish. What it means is that originally they did not constitute part of shiatsu and that most styles do not use them.

Namikoshi shiatsu does not use any diagnosis based on oriental medicine while Masunaga uses diagnosis via the abdomen (called hara diagnosis), but both styles accept that shiatsu is "treatment and diagnosis combined", meaning that, as practitioners, we are all the time feeling what the body of the receiver is telling us, and adapt our pressure and our treatment to what we feel in the body as a whole and in individual areas of the body.

Namikoshi shiatsu places the hands for thumb and palm pressure in a slightly different way than Masunaga shiatsu does, but both are based on using exclusively the weight of the body to apply pressure.

Namikoshi shiatsu, in its most basic form, repeats an exact number of times the pressure applied to individual points, while Masunaga shiatsu tends to press most points only once, but it can be still the same type of pressure.

Heisei shiatsu was derived from the common aspects of all shiatsu styles. But it has done something which, I believe, nobody has done before, or at least not to the extent we have, which is to put the emphasis on quality of pressure and relegate the theory to a second plane. Other shiatsu practitioners and teachers, with whom I have been in contact, have also developed ways to gauge and improve and pay attention to quality of pressure, but to my knowledge, these teachers still place as much importance on the theory as on the quality of pressure.

In Heisei Shiatsu we believe the *intensity* and *quality* of pressure are the two most important aspects of shiatsu, and we believe that the way to achieve the best results is not to go deeper into yet more theoretical constructs, but to go back to basics.

Empathy

After what I have said, it might be believed that I have implied that being a shiatsu practitioner is purely a question of technical knowledge. It would be wrong to assume that to acquire the best possible quality in the pressure we apply in a shiatsu treatment comes exclusively from learning a technique. As happens in all forms of bodywork, our attitude and awareness, the way we feel and empathise with receivers are as important as the technique. We take that to be a given.

You should not be in a caring profession unless you are ready to care for your patients. As one of the shiatsu mottoes says 'The heart of shiatsu is like maternal love'.

Technical skill devoid of empathy and ability to change pressure and way of treating according to the body and sensitivity of the receiver could almost equally be applied by a machine. Not quite, because even those who are not as caring as they should be in these professions feel more than what a machine can. This is one of the reasons why I am nonplussed when I read some research papers on acupressure which measure the force of pressure by having a practitioner apply pressure on weight scales.

Scales are obviously not muscles, and the reaction of hard metal or plastic to our pressure cannot be compared to the reaction of muscles. But, more importantly, it is obvious that it misses completely the qualitative aspects of pressure.

Chapter 2

Would you believe it?

Deep is not the same as hard or strong

When I teach 'Introduction to shiatsu' courses, I usually ask participants to tell the class if they know something about shiatsu or other bodywork modalities. The answers are many, some compare it to acupuncture, others to Tui Na, and some simply think that it is massage done through clothing without oils or creams.

But, everyone appears to be astonished when I explain that deep does not equate hard, that in fact, hard pressure tends to be shallow, because the muscles react by contracting, while deep pressure that is soft and fluid lets the muscles reach a deeper form of relaxation.

I also explain that it takes time to acquire this type of pressure and that at the beginning we all 'push' instead of 'press', meaning that we use our strength instead of letting pressure flow effortlessly from leaning in a relaxed way with our bodies.

In Heisei Shiatsu, quality of pressure is not incidental or subsidiary, it is the basis of what makes shiatsu unique. I can, in the same treatment, stimulate the transmission of nerve impulses that can balance the sympathetic and parasympathetic nervous system, produce a deep relaxation effect, improve breathing and activate muscles. I can help with pain issues and make the person come out of a session as if they were floating (their words, not mine). How profoundly these effects are achieved depends on how deep our pressure is. If our deep pressure is the opposite of forceful or vigorous, if it is at the same time painless, as it is in Heisei shiatsu, the relaxation effect is much more profound.

Dispelling the myth

There is a problem I have encountered so many times that I can't remember all the occasions. The problem arises from the meaning each person, practitioner, receiver or lay person attaches to the word "pressure", and from the many myths and misconceptions surrounding shiatsu. "Pressure" sounds like something ominous, something you want to be rid of in daily life, so unless one has experienced it as something pleasurable – as it can certainly be in shiatsu – one may perceive it as negative. This problem is compounded by the fact that many practitioners in the field of manual therapy associate shiatsu as a "hard" or "strong" practice, even when most of them have never received a shiatsu treatment. They also believe that if you go deeper, you cause pain or the pressure applied is harder. This is certainly the case among some shiatsu therapists, but I believe they are not the majority.

It is true that certain "styles" of shiatsu believe in fighting yang with yang, i.e. in pressing hard (I said hard, not deep, remember they are not synonymous) when you encounter painful or sore areas. In Heisei Shiatsu we believe the opposite, pain causes muscles to contract, not to relax. Sometimes, you can relax muscles if you let go of the pain, and although this is an interesting and beneficial development, it is not a necessary one except in very few cases. It is possible to relax skeletal muscles with soft but deep pressure.

Muscles need energy in the form of adenosine triphosphate (ATP) both to contract and to relax. Tightness, stiffness and muscular pain may lead to permanent or semi-permanent contracture and shortening of muscles with the corresponding increase in the expenditure of energy, as well as increasing the mechanical stress on proximal joints.

Although painful treatments may be as effective in improving the condition of contracted muscles, pain during treatments may put off some people who have become accustomed to their usual chronic pain.

As we shall see, it is not difficult to give a painless shiatsu, but it sometimes implies to let go of certain misconceptions about how we can exert force. Helping muscles to relax, and not be in a permanent state of tension, will also increase our energy levels, since we won't be using the extra energy needed to maintain chronic muscular pain or stiffness.

The physics of shiatsu

The human body is not a rigid structure. Even bones have more elasticity than metal. It is therefore strange, even peculiar, to see how pressure is measured in some research studies on acupressure. Some of these studies measure the intensity of the pressure applied by having the therapists press on scales, and then, somehow, transferring that pressure to specific points on the body of receivers.

This misses so much about pressure that it is difficult to know where to start. The first and most important thing it misses is quality. Metal or plastic scales cannot give us feedback on whether pressure is hard or soft, shallow or deep, pleasant or painful. It can only measure – and in my opinion not very accurately – intensity. But intensity on the surface of the body would not be the same as intensity on a rigid surface. When we press in shiatsu, we are listening to the body. We are feeling what that particular body, even that particular area of that body is telling us. Is it a sore area? Does it have painful memories? Pressure is *adjusted*, or at least, it should be adjusted to those sensations.

To this listening to the body, we add the feedback that comes from the subjective sensations of the person who is experiencing our treatment. No two bodies are alike, and people will have very different sensations from the same stimulus.

Giving shiatsu is not a mechanical action that could be replicated by a machine. How the practitioner uses his/her body and adapts to the body of the receiver are all part of the quality of pressure.

The second thing it misses is something we have been saying all along. One *does not apply* any force in shiatsu. One does not push or exert any pressure on the body. This is what seems to be the most difficult point to get across for those who have not studied shiatsu, and this is the reason why many blithely compare any type of pressure or force applied with what shiatsu does. This is why there is so much confusion in the research literature, where, in many cases, they take for granted that "pressure" means exactly the same in all instances when it does not. The shiatsu therapist just lets go of the body, just leans without pushing or exerting force and *without the intention* of pushing. I shall talk later about intention in shiatsu, and how, although our intention is important, the act of pressing is effortless leaning, effortless movement.

Incidentally, I am not the only shiatsu therapist to point out in a book the fact that the therapist does not use force, that in fact, the use of force in shiatsu is counterproductive leading to painful pressure for the receiver and making it harder on the body of the practitioner. Quite a few others say the same thing but, I believe I am one of the very few who puts so much emphasis on this since I think it is not only one of the most important aspects of good shiatsu practice but what differentiates shiatsu from other techniques[6].

When massage therapists who do not know much about shiatsu observe me working, they usually call my work "compressions" and say compressions are part of massage. I need to point out once more that it is very different. They partly believe it is similar because they are looking at my hands and not at what I do with my body.

---

[6] I have not read all the books there are on shiatsu. I have read quite a few and the only one I know of which expands on this attribute of shiatsu is the French book: Bel, I., 2022. *L'Esprit du Shiatsu*. Éditions Chariot d'Or.

They fail to observe the rocking movement of my body that is the initiator of my "pressure". The distinction is that they compress with their hands and I do not use the strength of my hands at all.

This is why my pressure and theirs is felt by both the therapist and the receiver as something completely different. This is why the therapeutic and relaxation effects are not the same.

Pressure in shiatsu comes from the Newtonian principle of action/reaction. When I let go of my body weight, the receiver's body gives way to my pressure to a certain point where it starts to react and press back against my hands, fingers, etc. As we shall see in a later chapter, this is why, to acquire a good pressure, the speed and rhythm with which we enter and leave, with which we start and stop pressing, are so important. Sudden, abrupt movements would simply startle the receiver who would tense up instead of relaxing. The action/reaction of applying pressure with the relaxed weight of the body is also the reason why, as therapists, we need to listen to the body of the patient, to know, or rather to feel, when it is appropriate to go any further or to stop. This too is why we need to give shiatsu on a futon or a table (or similar). Pressure applied in the air, without any resistance from something stopping the receiver's body from moving, cannot be as deep.

Deep and hard (or strong) are different things, and so are soft and shallow

I think that, by now, it will be clear that hard and deep pressure are two different things. An abrupt movement, a too fast application of pressure or a non-relaxed therapist can all result in hard pressure. Hard pressure is usually shallower because our bodies stiffen and will try to reject what is felt as invasive.

Softer pressure, on the other hand, can go much deeper since our body will feel it as something pleasurable, something which we want to feel in its entirety. But we need to be careful not to confuse soft with shallow in our daily practice. In many occasions, therapists seem to be afraid of going as deep as possible, and although their pressure is not hard, it is not deep either. As explained in the introduction, it is in fact frustrating for a receiver when pleasurable pressure stops short before it can be fully felt.

Is Heisei shiatsu a type of medical shiatsu?

The answer, as usual, is not straightforward. The answer is yes and no. Yes, it is medical shiatsu; all styles of shiatsu are medical, if, by that term, we understand we can treat health-related conditions such as back pain, neck stiffness, PMT, etc. It is not medical in the sense that we do not diagnose from the medical point of view. I do not diagnose a disk hernia, you need a scan to diagnose it. I cannot diagnose migraines, and doctors depend on your answers to certain questions to diagnose these. This doesn't mean that I never talk in Western medical terms. I have told quite a few people that they had scoliosis.

Sometimes it is very clear, but there are postures that make it easy to see. However, as I tell them, the only way to be 100% sure is to have X-rays. Whether they choose to confirm the scoliosis with X-rays or not, I still can recommend exercises and adapt my treatment to the condition.

Case history:

what you see is not what you get

I was one day at the hospital talking to the other volunteers, massage therapists, reflexologists and reiki practitioners, none of which were shiatsu therapists. We were talking about the different therapies we practised, and at one point the conversation turned to shiatsu and, after I had tried to explain in words what is the real meaning of "pressure" in the context of shiatsu, I was asked to demonstrate.

I was sitting next to one of the reiki therapists and started to demonstrate what I meant when I say that deep and hard are different. I first pressed on her leg with my usual pressure, deep but soft.

When I pressed the second time, I did the opposite, I pressed hard and strong. When I pressed hard, two of the other therapists said to our receiver – without any prompting from me – that the second hard pressure looked deeper. The reiki practitioner "testing" my pressure said no, the first one was deeper.

You can see depth once you are trained, but, generally speaking, it is the opposite. Hard looks deep but it is not. Soft looks shallow, but it doesn't have to be.

Chapter 3

What beginners do

Better the whole weight than half the weight

The first day of teaching always involves a degree of déjà vu for the teacher. Not only of having seen it in other students, but also because it reminds us of how we started out to learn shiatsu. Learning shiatsu is not that different as learning other tasks that require coordination of different parts of the body and which usually need the expert coaching of a teacher. When one learns to ski, the body is stiff at the beginning, it is difficult to relax even when the instructor tells us to do so. When we are complete beginners, learning to drive a manual car, it almost appears impossible to believe that one day remembering to use the clutch, the accelerator and the gear stick without forgetting the steering wheel at the same time will become natural. But it does. So let me put the mind of anyone who may doubt their abilities at rest. Everyone can learn shiatsu. It is not a complicated skill to learn. Of course, each technique or skill has its own learning timetable and its own peculiarities. As is the case in any new skill, when one learns shiatsu, there are physical and mental aspects. The mental aspect consists mostly of concentration. We need to concentrate on what we are doing and on what we are feeling. I will give a few tips on how to maintain concentration in chapter 7.

The physical aspect has some counterintuitive aspects, one of which is particularly noticeable with beginners. To follow with a previous analogy, when we begin to learn skiing, we are told we need to lean forward to avoid falling even when the body is telling us to do the opposite, to lean backwards. The most counterintuitive aspect of shiatsu is how far to lean with the body when applying pressure. There are far fewer chances of our pressure being painful or uncomfortable if we let go of the *whole* weight of the body. It is precisely when we control the movement and we stop it that our pressure can be unpleasant or even painful. Stopping the movement midway, as beginners are prone to do, is also more tiring for the practitioner. In other words, it is more difficult to relax, more difficult to make it a natural movement. But beginners are afraid to hurt the receiver and our instinct tells us to stop the movement. If I am lying down experiencing the movement of a particular student, nearly always I have to tell them not to be afraid and lean forward as much as possible.

The position of the arms, the hands and the fingers is important too, and it affects the quality of the pressure applied in shiatsu, but it is the movement of the body first and foremost which influences how pressure is perceived by receivers. In this respect, when teaching beginners, I ask people to pay more attention to the movement of my body, and invariably, they pay more attention to what I do with my hands. I did too when I began to study shiatsu. And, as I say, although the position and movement of the hands and arms is important, it is much easier to make those naturally than letting go with the whole weight of the body. Remember – except for a few exceptions – the whole weight is better than half the weight.

Our intention affects movement

Letting go of the whole weight is probably the most important part of acquiring a nice, relaxed effective movement in shiatsu which will result in a pleasant, painless and deep pressure. It is not enough though. There are other aspects of the movement which are also essential both to avoid any strain when we are working and to apply the best possible pressure. These aspects are learned with time. It is not possible to pay attention to everything one should be doing from the beginning, and different people have difficulty with different features of a skill in the process of learning it.

There are two other essential characteristics of how to move the body in shiatsu, and they are interconnected. It is almost impossible to do one without doing the other. The correct movement in Heisei Shiatsu originates from the solar plexus and ends with the awareness of the solar plexus over the area we are pressing. The movement of our body can be done in a very mechanical way or with intention, and intention is a very important feature of all bodywork. Our intention affects how we move, the same as the perception of our own body can affect posture.

Hips and solar plexus move together. The actual movement I am referring to cannot be easily explained in words, it has to be demonstrated and corrected by someone who can observe it. Even when I have demonstrated the movement and explained the common mistakes most beginners make before we start the practice, it is a bit difficult – because it is not a short process – to correct *minor* problems in the way we move in just a few days. But although these problems are minor – in the sense that are usually only perceptible to those who know what they are looking for – they can cause a lot of damage to our bodies, since small repetitive movements done in the wrong way are usually responsible for many of modern-day injuries due to overuse or bad use of our muscles, thus the name repetitive strain injuries.

One of the problems is the tilting of the hips. In some instances, practitioners tilt the hips forward too much when leaning towards the receiver's body, causing a break in the alignment of the practitioner's back which decreases depth of pressure and strains the lower back, and at other times one of the hips moves slightly further than the other, causing a lateral twist of the whole spine. Leaning forward to let our weight do the work, when we are kneeling or close to a massage table is mostly a movement of the hips.

Although it is the hips that move forward (and backwards when we stop pressing), the *intention* of the movement focuses on the solar plexus. If we think that the solar plexus is going to move together with our arms, and that the force we are going to apply is due to the solar plexus being above our hands or fingers, being above the point or area which I want to treat, which I want to press, it will be more difficult to push the pelvis forward or to tilt the hips to one side. Getting this movement right not only produces the maximum possible depth of pressure but it also helps with one of the characteristics of shiatsu pressure, perpendicularity. The three basic aspects of pressure in shiatsu are usually described as perpendicularity, concentration and maintenance.

Your height matters and other tips

To a great degree, in my initial teaching years, I followed the prescribed positions from my training both as a shiatsu practitioner and as a shiatsu teacher. Some of the changes I have made to the original way or form in which I was taught shiatsu, have come about because my students did something the "wrong" way. By "wrong", I mean that it was not the way I had taught them to do something. Of course, some of these mistakes are the common mistakes of which I have been talking about and the students need to be corrected, but other times, it made me wonder if the "mistake" was not in fact a better way of doing a particular task. Others have come about because I realised some students were struggling. I have always tried it any changes by myself and had a few students do the same. Then I asked for feedback from the person giving and the person receiving. The conclusion from these changes is that there is not one single way of giving shiatsu, even within the same style, we need to adapt it to our bodies. You should pay attention to your height and the natural way your body adapts to how we press.

This, for example, applies to how we place our hands and fingers. Some of us have more flexibility in the wrists and fingers than others, and the anatomy of our hands is not the same, some hands are bigger than others, for example. The clearest example of this is when we use the thumb. According to all shiatsu textbooks and styles, the thumb should not be flexed, but extended when applying pressure with it. This does not mean that it should be rigid or make an exact straight line. Some thumbs will bend backwards because the carpometacarpal joint is more flexible, while in other cases it would appear as slightly flexed. All are correct as long as it is adapted to one's own thumb anatomy so that it does not lead to injury or discomfort.

Case history: how my teaching changed

One day I was teaching how to apply pressure between the spine and the shoulder blade in the half-kneeling position – the one I had always taught previously – when I realised that one of my students, who was quite short, was struggling. On impulse, I asked him to try and do the same but, instead of half-kneeling, to kneel with both knees. Both he and I noticed immediately the difference, and realised that this position was much easier for him than the one I had been trying to teach him and saw that his back was straight. Quite a few attempts at changing the position for everyone and a lot of feedback later, I reached the conclusion that the best body position for a giver depended on their height. Generally speaking, taller persons were more comfortable and had the back straight when half kneeling, while it was better for shorter persons to have both knees on the floor. From that moment on, I have always told students they can choose whichever of these two positions they find the easiest. What is clear, is that giving them a choice makes it easier, and, consequently, their pressure improves.

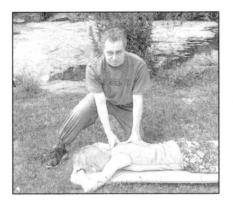

Half-kneeling position

Kneeling position

Chapter 4

Ways of pressing: our body as a tool

To apply pressure in shiatsu you can use the palms of your hands, your thumbs, your fingers, the elbows and the knees, and some therapists also use their feet. The vast majority of therapists, however, use mainly the fingers, the thumbs and the palms of the hands, with the clarification that the thumb is the main "finger" used.

Depending on style of shiatsu, they are used slightly differently. Namikoshi Shiatsu uses the hands together with one thumb over the other thumb, and the palms are most of the time used together too, while Keiraku or Zen Shiatsu normally leaves one hand stationary while the other presses either with the thumb or with the palm of the hand.

Before we establish the particular way in which we use all of these in Heisei Shiatsu, let's see the advantages and disadvantages of using the thumb, the palm of the hand or other parts of our body.

Thumb over thumb

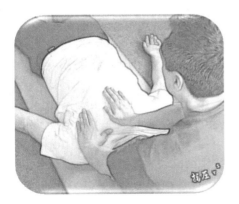

One hand stationary while the other applies pressure

The thumb

The main disadvantage of using the thumb is the muscle stiffness it causes, mostly around the base. The thumb in our daily life, obviously, is not used to apply pressure, and the muscles resent it at the beginning (the three thenar muscles). Like in many human activities, it is only a question of time and practice before the muscles become strong and adapted enough to their new function so that they do not feel tight or achy after applying shiatsu with the thumb. It is not such a big discomfort that stops one from doing any other activities, it lasts for maybe a couple of hours after giving a shiatsu, and personally, I do not remember it lasting more than a couple of months in which I must have given about ten long shiatsu treatments. An ex-student of mine told me that after graduating he was doing mostly massage, so that when he started working with shiatsu again, he felt the stiffness again for about a couple of weeks.

On the other hand, the advantages of using the thumb as one of the main tools to apply shiatsu pressure are many. Our fingertips are very sensitive to touch, much more so than our arms or legs. All fingers have sensory nerve endings which allow for the sense of touch and the discrimination of shapes, textures, and objects. Each fingertip has over 3,000 touch receptors, many of which respond primarily to pressure. Using the thumb or the fingers instead of the elbow or the palm of the hand has the distinct advantage of allowing us to feel more the sensations emanating from the body we are pressing, as well as from particular muscles and areas of the body. It allows us to diagnose more easily from the point of view of shiatsu.

The thumb, as compared to the fingers, has more mobility and can be placed at different angles in relation to a point on the body. It can lie from flat with the whole thumb touching the body to almost completely vertically with several degrees of inclination in between. This variation in inclination is one of the procedures we use to increase or decrease the intensity of our pressure.

Because of its smaller surface in comparison with other body parts such as elbows or knees, it is very useful to apply more focused pressure when we want to reach certain points. With other parts of the body we would be pressing too large an area.

This can be seen or rather felt when we press on the (anterior) sacral foramina.

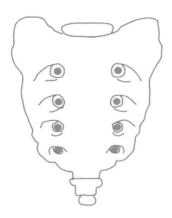

Sacral Foramina; bladder 31, 32, 33 and 34 in meridian terminology;

上髎 (じょうりょう top hip bone),

次髎 (じりょう second hip bone (literally next hip bone)),

中髎 (ちゅうりょう middle hip bone),

下髎 (げりょう bottom hip bone).

It should be pointed out that 髎 is an old kanji only used nowadays in the context of acupoints

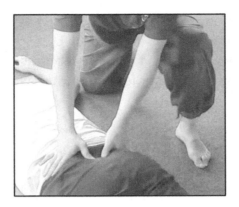

Pressing on the sacral foramina with anything but the thumbs would not be as focused on the points we want to reach.

When using the thumb to apply shiatsu pressure, the four fingers serve as support, which makes the thumb pressure softer, more accurate and can create a "cushion" in certain areas of the body, especially in the arms and legs.

And finally, learning how to use the thumb in different ways facilitates working in special or more difficult circumstances. For example, when I need to work on the feet with someone who is in a wheelchair or sitting and finds it difficult to move. In such an instance, my posture is not going to be ideal, so I have to find creative ways to be able to still give shiatsu in these situations.

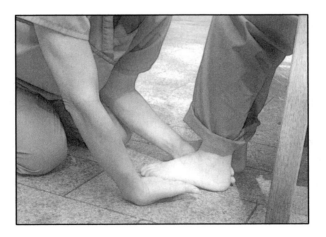

Two images of how I need to adapt when the person is not mobile, I don't want to ask them to move to the bed because that would cause pain, and I want to work on their feet.

The thumbs and fingers in Heisei Shiatsu

From the previous paragraph you may have guessed that we use thumb pressure a lot in Heisei Shiatsu, and you would be completely right. We hardly use thumb over thumb pressure because it is very difficult to apply pressure exclusively with the bottom thumb as you are supposed to do. The solution is to work with one thumb next to the other and distribute the pressure between both of them. This leads to work with both hands as one unit, to an easier way of applying pressure and to covering a slightly bigger surface area to press on. We do use both hands together more often than having one hand stationary while the other works although we do the latter as well. Working with both hands together makes having a good posture easier, especially when the receiver is taller than us, and to have a more focused pressure, something that we believe it is important to increase the neurostimulation of the mechanoreceptors under the skin.

There is a theory in some shiatsu circles that working with hands together is what results in painful shiatsu treatments. In spite of the theory that you need your two hands working separately so as not to cause pain, I am absolutely certain that I have proved to myself, to my students, and to all my patients, that this is not the case, and that if you know how, you can apply painless pressure with thumbs next to each other and hands working in unison. In fact, I am confident that it is the incorrect use of the weight of the body that in most cases leads to pain being caused during a shiatsu treatment. Whatever the cause of the pain that might be felt during a shiatsu session, the reason is certainly not that you use the two thumbs and hands next to each other.

But we do not always use both hands together in Heisei Shiatsu. For practical reasons, it would be very difficult to access certain areas of the body, such as the neck, if we were to work with both hands together.

There is nothing wrong with working sometimes with the hands in unison and other times with one hand stationary and the other moving. Both are valid ways of applying shiatsu.

The four fingers are used much less than the thumb to press directly in Heisei Shiatsu, although they play a critical role in supporting thumb pressure. When pressing, the four fingers are normally used together as one unit, for example when working on the face, or finger over finger when working on some specific points such as Large Intestine 20 which I have used quite a few times to clear blocked noses.

Large Intestine 20 迎香 (げいこう welcome fragrance)

The palms of the hands

Palm pressure is in general less acute than thumb pressure, so it can be used for a number of reasons. Since the palms have a larger surface area than the fingers and are usually warmer, they can be used as a preparation for the thumb pressure that may follow or as a warm-up of an area that might be tight or cold when the patient has just arrived. It also gives us the opportunity to begin feeling the muscles and body of the receiver and gauge the tension or lack of in each area.

Palm pressure is more suited to cases of swollen arms or legs (oedema) whether due to simple fluid retention – as happens in most cases – or because of pregnancy or medication.

The exception to *any type of pressure* is when the oedema is due to a blood clot which would be a contraindication for any touch therapies.

I also use palm pressure to make the breathing deeper and slow the rate of respiration, in other words, to calm down the breathing and thus the whole person. It can be done when pressing the back or pressing the abdomen. I shall explain later in the chapter on abdominal shiatsu how to help people breathe more deeply.

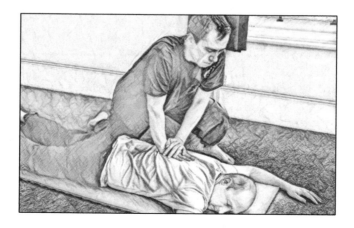

Palm pressure to increase depth of breathing

Elbows and knees

The elbows and knees are used much less by Heisei Shiatsu therapists. Both are used when you want to apply very strong pressure, which I hardly ever do. I do it occasionally, when I believe certain muscles would benefit from that kind of pressure. The way I do it is very controlled, for example, I only use the knees, in a tiny number of cases, on the hamstring muscles and I am very careful so as not to cause any pain, I am careful not to push with the leg at all and to let go of my weight only to a certain point.

In the very few cases that I do this, it is because I am faced with a difficult case of chronic backache which has not responded to my usual treatment as explained in chapter 9.

Characteristics of pressure

The effect pressure has on the body varies according to many conditions, the type of body of the receiver, the shape of the thumb and fingers of the therapist and many more, including the temperature of the room. We are here concerned about what we, as therapists, should know of the characteristics of shiatsu pressure to improve its quality. The three characteristics that everyone in this field agrees on are that pressure should be perpendicular, stationary and sustained.

Depending on the shape and area of the body we are working on,
perpendicularity changes the direction of our pressure

We always apply pressure perpendicular to the point or points we are working on at that precise instant. Sustained pressure refers to the fact that we always hold the pressure even if it is for the briefest of moments. What we don't do is exit immediately after having reached the adequate depth. Pressure in shiatsu is stationary, meaning that we do not circle, we do not knead as done in massage.

As useful and common-knowledge as these three prescriptions are, there are three further characteristics which are much less talked about in shiatsu, but in my opinion, just as important, namely intensity, frequency and speed. Frequency refers to the number of times we press on a particular point, set of points or area of the body. We can press once, twice or as many times as we think appropriate. The effects of varying our speed are explained in chapter 6.

By intensity we mean, at least in Heisei Shiatsu, how deep our pressure goes. Intensity and frequency are connected. When we are working on someone, the deeper we can go, the fewer times we need to press again and vice versa. When we encounter a situation or a person that cannot receive deep pressure what we need to do is to go over the points or area several times more often than usual to produce a deeper effect.

Case history: when I take criticism of my shiatsu from other shiatsu therapists as high praise

I once exchanged shiatsu treatments with another shiatsu therapist I knew. After finishing my treatment, she said she had never received such a deep treatment or pressure, not even when she was in Tokyo. I asked, as is my custom, if it had been painful or pointy or uncomfortable at any time, and she replied no.

She, however, said that no compatriots of her would accept or like my type of treatment. Although I already had a few regular clients from her country, I chose to say nothing.

The peculiarity of this exchange – at least from my point of view – is that she was making the comments as a criticism.

As if having a deep, painless pressure was bad and not going to be accepted or liked, or even something that could be good or useful in the context of shiatsu.

I could only take it as high praise.

Did she mean that my pressure was deeper than anything she had tried in Japan?

That my painless pressure could go deeper than the Japanese practitioners she had tried?

High praise indeed!

Chapter 5

I can repeat it
a thousand times …

but I cannot say it clearer

This chapter includes a couple of activities that consist of watching short excerpts from videos. You can skip the activities if you don't want to break the continuity of the story, but I recommend reading the activities section even if you don't do them because it illustrates the point I am trying to make in this chapter. You can go back and watch the videos at any time.

I cannot say it clearer

It doesn't matter how many times I repeat it, I cannot say it clearer. Books, manuals, videos, teachers, research papers and even shiatsu therapists, many of them say that because body points you work on coincide, because the points you press may have different names but most of them are found in the same location, then therapists are basically doing the same thing, as if the action of your whole body, or whether you use tools, or which tools you might be using while working on those points didn't make any difference. Some even call shiatsu "ischaemic acupressure". Some even go as far as saying that "These systems [shiatsu, acupressure, myotherapy, neuromuscular therapy] differ mostly in their theoretical models and not in the way pressure is applied to the client's body"[7].

---

[7] Lowe, W.W., 2009. *Orthopedic massage: Theory and technique.* Elsevier Health Sciences.

They ignore completely the quality of your pressure, whether you use your strength or your body weight, whether the transfer of weight from your body is done in a relaxed manner or not, whether you circle the point or your pressure is stationary as if none of that mattered. So you have teachers[8] and books which are used as evidence for complementary therapies[9] blithely claiming that who cares if your pressure is pleasurable, soft and deep and produces a deep state of relaxation or it is painful, impossible to enjoy and makes your muscles ache for two days. They touched the same point(s) didn't they?

You might as well say that trigger point therapy, acupressure, shiatsu, acupuncture, driving a nail with a hammer through your body, sticking a drawing pin inside someone or hitting the point repeatedly with your knuckles are all the same therapies. If it is the same point what difference could it make? We might as well use a screwdriver and a hammer.

As you can imagine, I must disagree entirely. The difference, the *practical* difference is not only which tool you use but, if you use your body, i.e. your thumbs, fingers or elbows, _how_ you press (we are not talking about possible theoretical differences). It is not the same thing, in terms of either perception or effect, to use the strength of your arms than to transfer your weight. It is not the same when I *only* use the transfer of my weight as when I use it *in part* and I *also* use the strength of my arms or hands. Even when the same words are used for what one should do – to lean with the body – if you pay attention, the action is not the same. It is very easy to spot once you know what to look for. And no, I do not mean the slight differences of individual actions, I mean very clear differences in all those who practise the same technique.

---

[8] https://www.youtube.com/watch?v=myZ4qWwd9Zo

[9] Mac Beckner, W. and Berman, B., 2003. *Complementary therapies on the Internet* (Vol. 1). Churchill Livingstone. This book was used quite a lot for the Review of the Australian Government Rebate on Natural Therapies for Private Health Insurance.

To write this chapter, I have had to rely on conversations with other therapists, practical demonstrations of trigger therapy on myself, websites, research papers and excerpts from books that I have read, and videos I have watched. You have some of these in the reference section at the end of the book. I will give the URL for the videos and the timings when explaining the differences. Whether those videos will have been removed from the internet when you read this book is something I cannot know, but what I can do is assure you that you can see the same phenomenon in many other videos. Let me, for instance, point out the big differences between "pressing" in shiatsu and "pressing" in trigger point therapy.

To illustrate this point, I am going to compare short excerpts of videos of shiatsu therapy and videos of trigger point therapy and talk about the visible part of pressure before explaining briefly the aspects that can be felt by the patient and by a teacher.

If you look from minutes 42:34 to 43.26 on the following video https://www.youtube.com/watch?v=D-cHpT_UUog, you see the shiatsu therapist making ample movements of the hips in order to press the points on the back of the legs, and letting go of the weight of his body, while if you look from minutes 2:58 to 3:03 of a video of working on a trigger point in one of the calves on https://www.youtube.com/watch?v=BlqBGSTYaHs, you can appreciate that the movement, the letting go of the body is much smaller. This is, I believe, even much clearer when you look at how to press a point on the back in shiatsu, from 1:27 to 1:36 on https://www.youtube.com/watch?v=GxboaGJ0Oz8 as compared to what the therapist does in trigger point therapy, from 4:46 to 5:04 on https://www.youtube.com/watch?v=sGwo1xBBYoU where, although the therapist talks about leaning with the body weight and uses her body weight in part, it is not to the same extent as shiatsu therapists do. Moreover, she reinforces the application of mechanical force with the hand on the wrist or on the fist.

Trigger point therapy is also called ischemic compression and it is sometimes applied with tools.

Even if we leave aside the different qualitative aspects of pressure when using one's body from when one uses a tool, when looking at the video below, I think it is clear the therapist pushes the tool. He doesn't simply lean and let go of his weight as it is done in shiatsu. You can see the tool applied from 1:05 to 1:11 on https://www.youtube.com/watch?v=WXqBrsbrnWM.

None of this means that I believe trigger point therapy or any other therapy is in any way inferior to shiatsu or not as useful. This is certainly not what I am saying. What I am saying is that the two techniques are different, and that although they both use the word "pressure" they are talking about different things, and that although they might use the same points, because what they do with those points is *very* different, the only logical conclusion is that the techniques *are not* the same. Both are valid and useful techniques, the therapist simply uses his or her body in a different way, not better nor worse, differently.

The same can be said of the differences between Tui Na and Shiatsu. Just because they may share some theoretical aspects, it doesn't mean they are the same or felt the same by either therapists or patients. Chinese dietetics shares a lot of *theoretical constructs* with Tui Na and some styles of shiatsu such as the 5 elements or the circulation of energy via meridians. It doesn't follow that eating chicken liver is the same as pressing or working on a point.

There are of course individual differences on how practitioners of any therapy press, and one can feel differences between those who have studied with one particular teacher and others. However, even when one takes into account all these factors, it is easy to appreciate that therapies are not the same. I recently asked two therapists to find one of my trigger points on the arm and press it. I also asked another person to tell me the differences.

One of the therapists circled the point while the other didn't, but both went in quite quickly using their strength instead of entering gradually as done in shiatsu.

The invisible perception

The differences between shiatsu and trigger point therapy, and other therapies that might talk about pressure, which I have mentioned and illustrated with examples from videos and personal experiences are the ones that are immediately visible. There are other differences, more subtle and not as easily noticeable, but which I personally consider of paramount importance. I think these features of using one's own body can make the world of a difference in how your shiatsu is perceived by the receiver. Because whatever we say, however hard we demonstrate, the proof of the pudding is in the eating, and the proof of your shiatsu treatment is in what the person in your hands feels and experiences. Or in other words, shiatsu is a manual therapy based on touch. The perception of touch is seldom visible although there are sometimes signs in the expression of the face or the contraction of the feet.

I must repeat that this does not mean that one therapy is better than the other. We do not know – at least not until someone does some research and looks into it – whether the effects of different ways of pressing are similar or not, although, as I have said before, I believe deep painless pressure in shiatsu to be more effective, but bear in mind that I am comparing shiatsu with shiatsu not with other techniques. And in shiatsu it is not – or it shouldn't be in my opinion – the hands or arms that press or push, pressure does not come from the action of the hands and/or arms.

All of which simply leads to the question: what do hands, elbows and arms do in shiatsu if they don't push or press?

The answer is "not much", but what they do is still essential. As I explained in chapter 3, students, especially those who come from massage therapy, tend to look at the teacher's hands even when they are told that the movement of the body is more important.

Patients too have the same belief and I have heard many times "your hands must be very tired". My hands do not get tired because they do very little. My body doesn't get tired because all it does is a rocking movement. This is why shiatsu has been described as a lazy activity[10].

But hands do something in shiatsu. There are two main tasks for the hands and the crucial one for a nice, soft, deep pressure is to just be, to do nothing. When you lean towards your patient, your hands can be hard or soft. The softer and more relaxed they are, the more enjoyable your pressure will be. This, of course, extends to the arm and shoulders and the rest of the body for that matter. But somehow, it is more difficult to appreciate in the hands. I believe my students in shiatsu taster courses are a bit surprised when I put so much emphasis on softening their stance and thus their pressure. The other job the hands do has to do with how I position them. When using the palms, if I do not spread the pressure all over the hand and use the edges of the hand, pressure is very uncomfortable and hard. To avoid this, I need to know how to position my hand.

If I am applying finger or thumb pressure, the hands have a vital supporting role, how the hands adapt to the anatomy of specific parts of the body – always respecting the anatomy of the therapist's hands – also changes the quality of the pressure. In both cases, the fingers have a role. For finger or thumb pressure, the inclination or angle changes the perception of pressure. For palm pressure, putting the fingers together or separate changes the way we feel it. This also applies when using the elbow, how much we bend it and how we place it in relation to our bodies are factors that change our pressure.

_____

[10] Lundberg, P., 2009. *The Book of Shiatsu: Vitality & Health Through the Art of Touch*. Simon and Schuster.

Case history:

excruciating back pain at the hospital

I once treated a young man who had an inoperable tumour. He asked one of the nurses for a massage because he was in terrible pain. When I went to his room, it turned out that his pain was in the lower back just above the pelvis. There are several options to treat pain in Heisei Shiatsu. That day I decided to check which points in the area he had signalled were painful. We found a few painful points, some of them so tender that even light touch would make the patient jump. Although the pain moved slightly during my treatment – something that sometimes happen – I was able to pinpoint with some accuracy which were the most tender points. But, as you already know, I do not believe in adding more pain to what is already painful, so I never work directly on tender points except maybe sometimes with such a light pressure as to be almost imperceptible. Instead I worked on the area around painful points until both the patient and I were satisfied that pain had been reduced. I must confess it was a hard case both because of the intensity of the pain and because of its moving nature, but I persevered for about half an hour when there were still two or three painful points left from the initial ten or so.

The week after, I went to visit him again when his mother told me "I don't know what you did, but his back pain was almost gone and has never been as bad since then". I was pleased to hear it of course. The only problem being that he now had a painful arm although it was nothing compared to the excruciating pain he had been experiencing the previous week. Luckily, even when sometimes the area became painful again, the intensity was always much less than on the first day I visited him.

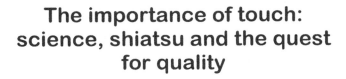

Chapter 6

The importance of touch: science, shiatsu and the quest for quality

Attitudes towards science

There are several different general attitudes towards science among the public, although I am more interested in explaining those attitudes in the world of complementary therapies, both from the therapists' and the users' point of view. There are, of course, many individual variations in the classifications I am making, with much overlap between the different groupings and the individual beliefs. Nonetheless, I believe these classifications are valid to understand attitudes towards science in this world – and in the world of shiatsu and other complementary therapies in particular – which may make us understand how to spread knowledge – instead of myths – about shiatsu.

There are roughly 3 groups. The first group explains that randomised double blind placebo control (RDBPC) studies are the "gold standard" in research and seem to give this explanation as justification for the lack of research in shiatsu or other manual therapies. At the same time, quite often, they accompany this explanation with another explanation saying the oriental view of health clashes with the Western view and point to this as one of the reasons for this gap in research.

I honestly do not know where to start. The RDBPC is only, exclusively, the gold standard when it comes to medicinal drugs and this comes with quite a few caveats. How on earth can you blind the practitioner of a manual therapy to what they are doing?

It is impossible in physiotherapy, yoga, Tai Chi, guided meditation, exercise, massage, shiatsu or any type of physical or face-to-face therapy. Even single-blind studies in these areas are very difficult to carry out. I have seen some studies that claim to be single-blind because the person taking the measurements did not know what intervention the patient had had, but most researchers would define single-blind when the receivers (the subjects in research parlance) do not know if they are getting the real treatment or not. In shiatsu in particular I only know of one such study in which the practitioners gave "sham" shiatsu by using the same points as in the actual shiatsu treatment but they did not use the weight of their bodies to apply shiatsu, or, as they put it, without any weight transfer, with only contact with the receiver[11]. It would be very interesting to observe how they managed to do it. The reason I ask this is because when one is accustomed to using the weight of one's body in treatments, you end up doing it subconsciously, you don't think about it. This type of single-blinding can of course only be applied to subjects that have never received shiatsu before. Can you imagine if every study on physiotherapy, exercise or massage had to be carried out with subjects that had not had any experience of those? Not easy, eh? Even then, the conclusions could hardly be generalised to the whole population. In fact, the discussion about what constitutes an adequate control for non-pharmacological interventions goes on.

---

[11] Bernardinelli, N., Valery, A., Barrault, D., Dorland, J.M., Palut, P., Toumi, H. and Lespessailles, E., 2023. Effectiveness of Shiatsu on Fatigue in Patients with Axial Spondyloarthritis: Protocol for a Randomized Cross-Over Pilot Study. *Rheumatology and Therapy*, pp.1-11.

You can, for example, read the appropriately titled research paper: "The Trials and Tribulations of Selecting Comparison Groups in Randomized Trials of Nonpharmacological Complementary and Integrative Health Interventions", where the author explains how it is not possible to administer a true placebo effect in psychotherapy, exercise or lifestyle interventions, and that it is even more challenging for complementary therapies[12].

But even RDBPCs come with caveats and, as researchers can tell you, they sometimes draw wrong conclusions from these studies. Often times, the wrong conclusions come from choosing an inappropriate placebo or from not taking into account that placebos can have both positive and negative side effects (called a nocebo when the effects are negative).

In any case, this attitude towards science forgets that science does not only investigate medicinal drugs, but also quality of life. It was scientists – not I or any "alternative" health practitioner – who came up with the concept of quality-adjusted life year (QALY), concept which of course has its critics, but which is used in health research. This is why my main criticism of this understanding of science is that science is not only about quantity but also about quality. For a more detailed discussion of some of the misconceptions and misunderstandings about evidence-based medicine in the world of shiatsu, please refer to 'Shiatsu, the Evidence Base. A critical review of a webinar' by Stergios Tsiormpatzis which is available online[13].

---

[12] Sherman, K.J., 2020. The trials and tribulations of selecting comparison groups in randomized trials of nonpharmacological complementary and integrative health interventions. *The Journal of Alternative and Complementary Medicine*, 26(6), pp.449-455.

[13] https://orientalmedicine.eu/images/Articles/2019-webinar-review.pdf

A second group views science as a series of facts that nobody can deny. I remember a friend of mine, with whom I have had quite a lot of conversations about all of this, who came one day with a sentence that still makes me laugh.

He said: "Because when the light is on is on and when it is off it is off". I did laugh then and it makes me laugh now. Everybody knows that whether they accept or believe in scientific explanations. Before Isaac Newton came up with his law of universal gravitation, *everyone* knew that apples fell down, people didn't believe apples went up when detached from the tree just because they didn't know about the force of gravity. What Newton did was come up with an explanation or interpretation for this fact. He did not come up with a new fact. This is what my friend fails to understand. He watches a programme on TV and takes it as gospel truth. If you know any scientists – and there are scientists in my family – they will tell you that in any congress they attend they do not agree on many things. Yes, science includes opinions and different interpretations of the same phenomena. No, science is not about incontestable facts. You do not hear scientists say: "this study has proven that...", they talk about hypothesis and suggestions and the evidence pointing to *possible* or *likely* conclusions.

This error and misconception of what constitutes science can even be seen more clearly if we think about what is an exact science. There is only one exact science which is mathematics. We could probably say that engineering approaches mathematics more than other disciplines. What I think is obvious is that anything related to biology or even more so to health is anything but exact. Before any intervention I do not know how successful or unsuccessful it is going to be. When the doctor gives you pills for non-specific back pain, they do not know if it is going to work. If it doesn't, they give you something else. All we can do is make use of statistics, which, of course, cannot possibly be of any consolation for the person who suffers from the pain and for whom the medication does not work.

This attitude to science – or a mixture of this and the first group's attitude – is frequently used by some complementary-medicine bashers who *pretend* to believe that evidence is what they chose to be at any particular time or discussion. In scientific parlance, they cherry-pick evidence to suit the conclusions they have already reached disregarding any evidence that contradicts what *they want* to believe. They talk as if there were no invisible things in modern Western medicine. Really? Why do you think it is called non-specific low back pain? What do doctors see to diagnose fibromyalgia? Nothing, that's the answer, they see nothing, it is invisible. How do they diagnose complex regional pain syndrome? What do they see in their machines? Nothing. Can migraines be seen on a machine or blood test? Not that I know of. They send you for a scan to discard certain possible causes of the migraines, not to diagnose migraines.

Yes, there are invisible things in modern Western medicine. I also think I should point out that my friend and many people from this group choose – even if they deny it – what to believe. When my friend sees a "scientist" criticising something he wants criticised, then it is scientific. When the same "scientist" criticises something that has helped him, such as acupuncture, then it is not scientific.

A third group views science as something that is very broad in scope, interesting and powerful but that it does not have the answers to everything in life or in the subject we are talking about here: health. Science cannot explain why one person reacted positively to chemotherapy and another didn't react at all. Science cannot explain why surgery is successful with one person but unsuccessful with another one. But this does not mean that science is not useful. On the contrary, we believe that evidence can help us improve our clinical expertise, but at the same time we know that evidence is no substitute for said clinical expertise. People in this group believe that to do good science, you have to doubt everything, including your ideas and your conclusions, or, if you want it to express it in another way nearer to the realm of shiatsu and other manual therapies, we are always learning.

You cannot stop learning if you are presented with new cases and challenges. There are no fixed facts like the second group believes, and there are no fixed explanations like the first group believes.

Yes, there is objectivity in my treatments, as when I see if a patient can move their neck more than before, or they report having slept better, but there is also subjectivity, from the patients, for example, when they report less pain, or that they feel as if they were floating, and from me, the practitioner, because I use my intuition. This is why I personally see no contradiction in using *at the same time* my knowledge of Western anatomy and physiology and my knowledge of Traditional Chinese Medicine (TCM).

Phenomena and health issues can have several different interpretations and all or at least some of them can be useful. You do not have to stick to one interpretation for it to be scientific. Sometimes I prefer one, sometimes a different one, and most times a mixture of interpretations. Does it work? In quite a few instances but not always, but I think it does work in more cases than if I use one of the more rigid interpretations found in the first two groups. Do I know in advance if it is going to work? Of course not. Do I sometimes follow the same procedure as with other patients that have come to me with the same problem? Of course I do, but I am open-minded, I do not know if it is going to work this time. In other words, I rely on the experience-based plasticity of the brain, because your brain is not a series of neurons that never change, any more than your genes determine your personality for life. So I observe what happens during my treatment and change it if necessary.

Touch and science

How does massage work? Why does massage (most massage at least) relaxes you and has a positive effect on muscles? Science knows not. Yes, that is right. One needs to realise that science can know that something is beneficial and that it helps and not know why, not know the mechanisms of why this happens. Abubakr Muhammad ibn Zakariyya al-Razi, better known as Rhazes, was a Persian doctor from the 9th-10th century who is considered the first one to have carried out clinical trials with control groups, but his experimental medicine methods do not seem to have taken hold for a long time. In the modern era, Dr James Lind, who apparently didn't know anything about Rhazes's work, is considered the first doctor to have conducted a controlled clinical trial to find a remedy for the terrible disease of scurvy. He discovered that oranges and lemons were the best remedy for that terrible disease but he had no idea why. This was discovered much later.

So, from a scientific point of view, many times, all we have are hypothesis of why something is beneficial. It is known that massage helps preterm infants gain weight, and that it is more effective with deeper pressure than with light touch. It is also known, both by science and by our own experiences, that a different quality of touch produces different sensations and perceptions. Try stroking your cat against the direction of the hairs instead of in the same direction if you don't believe me.

Under the skin we have a series of receptors that react to touch and pressure and which relay information to the brain. These sensory receptors are called mechanoreceptors and it is believed that they are activated during massage leading to relaxation and pain relief. Although classical massage and shiatsu are quite different, it is quite possible that both activate responses in the mechanorreceptors even if it is done in different ways. What is clear is that some parts of our body are more responsive and sensitive to touch because they have a higher density of mechanoreceptors, especially those that are responsible for fine discriminative touch, the Merkel cells. In some shiatsu styles this is in part the explanation for using more often the fingers or the thumb, because they may sense more than other parts of the body when we are touching the receiver.

From our point of view, what is important – apart from the beneficial effects – is that our brains contain touch maps that replicate this sensitivity with the hands, the lips and the tongue having the highest density of mechanoreceptors.

It is known that these maps are not set in stone for the rest of your life, they change. One of the clearest examples is seen in people who play musical instruments in which one hand necessitates more manual dexterity than the other. The touch maps are different for each hand.

Which leads us to one of the main theses of this book, that good quality of pressure can be acquired, can be learned, that even if your pressure is naturally hard, it is possible to soften it, that even if your pressure is too light and not deep enough, it is possible to make it deeper, that you can increase your sensitivity and thus know when someone needs and prefers lighter or deeper pressure, and that if our pressure is pointy and painful not only it is possible but you should also aim to make your pressure more enjoyable. More enjoyable pressure results in happier patients/clients and more effective treatments.

The quest for quality

If good quality shiatsu pressure has a positive effect on mechanoreceptors by stimulating them, then it is quite likely that these receptors send signals to the brain which in turn will signal back making muscles relax. As one can imagine, our body does not only contain receptors that react to pleasurable stimulation but it also contains another type of sensory receptors called nociceptors that react to pain. If we are going to forget about these and not care about whether our pressure is pleasurable or pointy, hard and painful, we might be activating the receptors that will signal the muscles to *contract* instead of relaxing.

I am a firm believer that in every profession, aiming for quality makes us better, more confident and self-satisfied professionals and persons. I think it is obvious that it also makes for more satisfied patients. The issue is how to define quality in a particular profession. I have chosen a path that it is not much talked about in the world of shiatsu or in the world of massage either.

Or perhaps I should say that this particular path has chosen me. In what way it has chosen me has mostly been already explained in the preface and will become even clearer after you read the last chapter. My experiences both as a teacher and a practitioner have led me to regard the quality of the pressure you apply the first and most important condition for this quest. As you can imagine, this is not exclusive to shiatsu, it also happens in the different modalities of massage. As I am told by some massage therapists, they were surprised during their exams, because examiners do not seem to take into consideration whether a particular therapist's massage is painful or not, it is as if that didn't matter to the receiver.

However, even taking that into consideration, I believe this quest for quality is more important in shiatsu. The reason for this is that acquiring a good pressure in shiatsu seems to take longer than in massage and especially the way to acquire a good pressure is perhaps more counterintuitive. In shiatsu there are a number of elements that need to be addressed, such as how relaxed your body is, how much you are able to let go and use your body weight and your intention.

Even when my shiatsu is not successful in, for example, alleviating pain, or improving range of movement, I hope it has at least led to an enjoyable and relaxing experience. Not everyone is going to prefer my technique or me as a therapist – or anyone else's for that matter – but I prefer not to be known as the practitioner of a painful hard therapy by those who have never tried my shiatsu.

I am not sure if this book will convince shiatsu practitioners – and especially teachers – to pay more attention to the quality of pressure and see if all of us together can improve the negative perception of shiatsu in certain circles. What I am sure of is that if we can work together in this direction the world of shiatsu will benefit, that shiatsu will be better known and its benefits more appreciated.

Chapter 7

Relax, your tension affects your treatment

Posture and pressure are related

When I want to try and test students' pressure, I usually do so lying face down so that they can work on my back. It is a position from which I cannot see their bodies very well although I occasionally turn my head to have a look, but this only allows me a partial view of the front of their bodies. But I can feel what they are doing. So they are usually amazed when, from that position, I tell them, for example, that they are tilting one of the hips laterally. They wonder – and ask me – how I can possibly know.

What happens next is that I get up, have someone else lie down and correct this particular student's posture. Usually, I have the same student lie down and make them feel the difference in pressure with a good posture and with the specific point I was correcting. It is at this moment that their question is answered, something I could not have done with words.

Posture and quality of pressure are related, they go hand in hand. A word of caution. In our endeavours to acquire the correct posture, especially a straight back that does not tilt forward or sideways, we might end up overcompensating, eliminating the natural curves of the spine and creating tension in the upper back and neck. I personally did precisely that at one stage in my learning. Luckily, I was capable of unlearning it relatively quickly and acquire a more relaxed natural posture. This tension in shiatsu usually manifests itself in raised or tight shoulders when leaning forward.

And tension – of whatever type or origin, be it physical or mental – while giving shiatsu, is transmitted to the receiver, typically in the form of pointy or hard pressure.

Pressure Intensity matters

Not all areas of our body have the same texture or feel. Some are more rigid, some harder, some more flexible and some softer. This is so naturally, depending on our constitution, and due to our own personal life circumstances, how we have grown up, what types of job or sports we have done, etc.

This means that not everyone needs the same pressure applied, and the same can be said for different parts of the body. Some parts of our body will take more pressure intensity than others, and these are not necessarily the same for other persons, even if there are some similarities since we all have human bodies. The difference in intensity is most noticeable when we work on the abdomen (hara in Japanese). Many years ago, I was conducting a workshop on how to treat constipation with shiatsu, when the subject matter was, because of the workshop dynamics, changed to abdominal pressure. The participants were amazed to see my assistant apply deep pressure on my abdomen. Some of them said they did not know it was possible to press so deeply. I was in turn amazed at their amazement. I was truly surprised nobody had tried to go any deeper than they usually did. So the workshop turned out to be on how to apply deep pressure on an area which is more delicate and which makes us feel vulnerable, probably because it provides access to so many internal organs. In fact, I have seen quite a few shiatsu schools in which the abdomen is used only for diagnosis, but it is hardly ever included in treatments.

In any case, during that workshop, I had to ask participants to lean forward more, to use all of their body weight, and make use of their arms, hands and fingers to reduce pressure intensity when necessary, and above all, to relax their shoulders.

You can see the video of several workshops I have run on pressing the abdomen in the reference section.

Intensity in shiatsu is mostly controlled by the position of our arms, hands and fingers, and by how relaxed our posture is. Flexing the elbows more and having the thumb or hand flatter against the body will reduce intensity, while more extended elbows and fingers or thumb at an angle will increase intensity. And this brings us back to the movement of our body when giving shiatsu.

The arms change position, I don't

As explained before, leaning forward letting go of the whole weight of the body is less tiring and produces less tension in our bodies than controlling the movement and stopping midway. In Heisei shiatsu there are three basic positions depending on which area of the body we are working on, and our body build. These positions allow us to apply pressure in and come out with a gentle, relaxed rocking movement which is, in my opinion, one of the essential aspects of a good shiatsu. Unfortunately, or fortunately, we need to introduce another counterintuitive characteristic of shiatsu. We can flex the elbows more or less depending on how much intensity the receiver needs, but the arms also need to move to apply pressure on different points in the area or line we are working on. The natural tendency is for us to move our body. This leads to, for example, us bending our back to the left or right when we are working from medial to lateral (from nearer to the midline of the body to one of the sides). To avoid this, we need to learn to keep the original position, repeat the same rocking movement without changing position, and simply move our arms and hands to the new points we want to press. It is not difficult, but I takes a bit of concentration to get it at the beginning precisely because it is counterintuitive.

Intention revisited

Intention is a double edged sword. So let us start with something that may sound paradoxical. Intention is necessary and not necessary. Let me explain. When learning shiatsu, most beginners feel, especially in certain positions, that they are not pressing enough, that they do not reach the receiver completely. I know I said that they tend to not use the full weight of the body, and it may sound like a contradiction, but it is not. They are afraid to use the full weight of the body and, at the same time, they think that just by leaning, pressure is not being applied. In other words, they want to push, to exert force. They feel, quite naturally, that pressure comes from applying force. This is at its most obvious when working perpendicularly to the body of the receiver.

When we work with our bodies at 90° to another person, we need to move our body very little in order to have a deep pressure. But we feel as if very little is being done, so beginners push hard. Interestingly enough, you can observe this attempt at pushing harder on the practitioner's face. When someone pushes hard, the face becomes a bit contorted, it is as if the intention to push is expressed through the face.

In this sense, we need to relax, to have no intention, to simply let our bodies lean even if slightly and not to force the intention of applying pressure, to let our bodies be water and let gravity do the work. But in another sense, we do need intention. As I said before, we need the intention of our movement to come from the solar plexus, but we also need intention to concentrate our energy, or if you prefer, our transmission of energy to the point or points we are about to press. We also need to focus our intention on what we want to achieve, where we want to arrive at, whether we would like to stimulate or release the areas or specific points we are working on. Intention needs concentration, concentration helps with intention, and the rhythmic movement of our body when giving shiatsu helps us concentrate. Once we have learned the basics of shiatsu, tension usually comes from losing our concentration, from letting our mind wander. Although it is inevitable that we are going to become less concentrated sometimes – hopefully very seldom – when it happens, when our mind wanders, this tension is felt by the patients. But we are also able to act on our awareness, and make these episodes of absent-mindedness in our treatments very short and quickly return to a relaxed state of concentration.

Case history: when students find it hard to relax

In quite a few of my introduction to shiatsu courses, couples come to learn the rudiments of shiatsu. In one of these occasions, the man found it really hard to relax the whole position, the shoulders, the arms and especially the thumb. The woman complained about his pressure being really hard. Although I always check their pressure, I don't do this until past half-way the lesson so as to give a chance for them to self-correct before I go on to a more individualised correction. In this case, I went to try his pressure by myself. What I felt when I was lying on the mat was that his whole body was tense. I had to repeat several times and work step by step for him to relax. 'Relax your shoulders', 'relax your arms, they are too rigid'.

Once he had relaxed a bit, I swapped places with another student, to help this man relax further with me instructing him while looking at his posture, etc. This last part was essential to have him relax the thumb. Many people find it difficult to relax the thumb, but, when you use it to transmit pressure and energy, this is of paramount importance.

Case history: toe rotations

When I teach toe rotations in professional courses, almost everyone does exactly the same thing I did when I was being taught. We rotate the patient's toes with our shoulder raised, which is the tensest position possible.

After a short while, I make them aware of that fact, and most of them relax the shoulders. I also explain to them that in Japan it is done differently. In Japan, they let you carry on with your shoulder raised until it gets too tired so you just let go. It is a harder way to teach and to learn, but very effective. You end up relaxing your shoulder naturally.

Notice the raised shoulder. A raised shoulder is in tension and that tension is transmitted to the patient. Compare the image with the one below.

Notice the relaxed shoulder.
It is less tiring for the therapist and more effective for the patient

Chapter 8

Speed & rhythm

Entering and exiting

When I wrote for a research paper the definition of shiatsu found in chapter 1 a few years ago, the co-authors of that paper and I discussed for a few weeks how to make the definition as precise and concise as possible. I believe the definition to be quite complete. Of course, no definition can encapsulate all the aspects of a manual therapy, or of anything else for that matter.

There is one point missing from that definition which we would have liked to incorporate, and which we discussed at length. In the end, we decided not to include it because we were unable to find an elegant way of doing so without breaking the flow of our definition. This aspect of shiatsu is rhythm and speed (tempo in musical or horse riding terms). Rhythm and speed in shiatsu are as important as depth and, to a certain extent, they are related. Traditionally, some of the masters spoke of three characteristics of pressure in shiatsu, perpendicularity, concentration and maintenance. Perpendicularity because pressure should be applied at 90°, concentration because our attention should be directed to the point(s) we are working on and maintenance because for shiatsu pressure to be effective, it needs to stay at the point(s) for a minimum of time, or in other words, we cannot exit very fast.

There are obviously many more characteristics of a good pressure. One of these is the speed with which we initiate and end one single pressure.

The speed *should* be the same for entering – from the moment you touch a particular point or area on the body until your pressure reaches its full intensity – and for exiting – from the moment you start to withdraw your pressure to the moment you stop touching a particular point or area.

It is, unfortunately, easier said than done. It is one of the aspects of shiatsu that takes a relatively long time to sink in, to be applied correctly. In fact, this is – in my opinion – one of the main reasons for shiatsu to take longer to learn than other techniques, but do not fret, everyone manages to get it, it simply takes time. The reason for the need for the same speed when applying pressure and releasing it, is – as far as I am aware – not known. It has been speculated that our nervous system gets contradictory messages if speed of entering and exiting are different, thus creating confusion. But what I *do* know is that when entering too fast pressure is *felt* as invasive, when exiting too fast, pressure is felt as stimulating in excess, as not relaxing, and when entering and exiting have different speeds, pressure is felt as uncomfortable. When I was a student, I had many conversations with the people receiving shiatsu from me, which included my classmates. We tried different ways of applying pressure and changing our speed and talked about how it was felt by both the practitioner and the receiver.

Good explanation of what constitutes speed when applying pressure? Maybe, but certainly not complete. There is another essential point, and I believe it is implicit in my explanation. Entering and exiting must be done *gradually*. Gradual application and withdrawing of pressure is fundamental if we do not want our pressure to be hard. As explained before, sudden, abrupt entering or leaving when applying pressure makes muscles tense up instead of relaxing. Speed may not alter the actual intensity of pressure, but it does alter the *perception* of intensity by our bodies, and this perception is extremely important for the comfort of the receivers.

Rhythm and speed

Rhythm is different from speed. Speed is how fast or slow you do something, while rhythm is the flow of our movements, how regular these movements are, what pattern they follow. Speed is related to how quickly we enter and leave a particular point or area of the body, while rhythm refers to how quickly (or slowly) we change from one point to the next, which in turn, is related to how long we keep pressing a particular point.

It is not usual to have the exact same rhythm in one treatment. This may be because we feel that different areas of the body need different rhythmic patterns, some need more concentration or staying longer on each point that I press, while others may benefit more from a quicker change of area or point of pressure. In my opinion, some areas of the body require naturally — in spite of their condition during the treatment — a slower or quicker rhythm, something that can equally be applied to individual persons.

Having said that, a (roughly) uniform rhythm in our treatments has a very beneficial effect on both the giver and the receiver. A steady rhythm results in a relaxed hypnotic state of mind that has been described by several of my patients as if they were floating. Part of our ability as shiatsu therapists comes from finding a balance between the general rhythm of a specific treatment and how we vary that rhythm during the same treatment.

Even when the rhythm changes from one area of the body to the next, the transition should be smooth, and above all, gradual. Graduality, as we have seen, is essential both for speed and rhythm. Shiatsu therapists should not go from a relative quick rhythm to a slow one and vice versa.

This rhythmic quality is derived from the non-verbal communication between the patient's body and ourselves as practitioners. And this is where empathy and our intention make their comeback to guide our treatments.

The empathy we feel towards the patients, and the intention to provide the best possible experience for them will allow us to find the most appropriate speed and rhythm and adapt our shiatsu treatment to the individual.

Adapt your shiatsu to the person

Diagnosis in shiatsu is usually defined as two complementary opposites: kyo (虚) and jitsu (実). These two concepts, and the idea that the best possible outcome is to achieve balance between the two, is also applied in some Japanese martial arts. In shiatsu, kyo is usually interpreted as absence of energy, emptiness, underactivity, while jitsu is defined as excess of energy, fullness, overactivity.

It should be clarified that neither is better than the other, this is why we look for balance, and that both terms are relative, they are not used in an absolute sense. A point, area or meridian is kyo (or jitsu) in relation to another point or area.

This is, in my opinion, one of the reasons why shiatsu is treatment and diagnosis combined. We are treating the person, but at the same time, we are trying to compare areas, points or meridians. There is no hard and fast rule to come to a diagnosis or conclusion based on these concepts. How the therapist feels on a particular day will change the perception too. I believe this is one of the reasons why we need empathy with the person being treated. Lack of empathy may result in us believing what we want to believe instead of listening to the changes that are taking place while we give our shiatsu.

This means that how we apply pressure should change, the speed, rhythm, how long we maintain the pressure and how deep we go should not be the same when we encounter kyo that when we encounter jitsu. As I said, there are no hard and fast rules and we should let our intuition guide us.

However, although I may change the way I press, in Heisei Shiatsu I still aim to go deep, in fact to go as deep as a particular point will let me.

If a point is kyo, it will let me go very deep, in some cases it is felt as a vacuum, and if the point is jitsu it will stop me from going as deep, but usually, little by little, even those points let me go deeper. Just because I slow down or speed up my rhythm there is no reason to stop applying deep, painless pressure.

Static holds

Sometimes, pressure cannot or should not be applied in certain areas of the body. We can still touch them.

The clearest example of this is during pregnancy. We do not press the abdomen when we are treating a pregnant woman, but I still lay the palms of my hands on each of the points/areas that I would normally press for a little while so that the mum to be and the foetus can feel the warmth, the energy and the connection. The calming effect of those static holds is noticeable, especially when the therapist pays attention to the quality of the connection through touch.

Incidentally, I call them static holds but I have heard other names such as holdings or no-pressure shiatsu. Although pregnancy is an example of when we would use static holds, there are other cases too. For example, people with certain diseases or conditions might find a change of routine distressing, and applying pressure may not be the most appropriate, especially in the first few sessions. This can happen because of strokes or in some cases of brain tumours. Static holds may also be suitable for patients who bruise easily because of health-related conditions.

Case history: speed change to reduce pain in difficult situations.

I once gave a few shiatsu sessions to an inpatient who had a fungal infection in the brain. His legs were swollen and painful and he had mobility issues. He could not get out of bed without help and he was losing the ability to walk.

Every time I went to his room, his girlfriend was there writing on her computer and attending to his needs when necessary. Because his legs were swollen, I applied palm pressure very slowly. It must have been the third or fourth session when he expressed his gratitude because my treatment was providing pain relief, something that, apparently, the medication failed to do. When he made the comment, his girlfriend was so surprised that had to ask him twice before she could ascertain that my treatment did help reduce the pain indeed.

Chapter 9

The no-pain principle

The no-pain principle

It is one of the basic principles of Heisei Shiatsu, if not *the* most important principle. I emphasise the practicality and benefits of this principle to both patients and students. How many times and to how many people have I had to explain that pain is not good! Why do so many people believe that pain is the solution, I don't know. But this is not the main point. The most important point of the no-pain principle is that, as well as making treatments much more enjoyable, it provides safety. The safety to work in almost any circumstance and with almost any type of patient. It is the mother of all precautions. Are you afraid to harm weak bones in osteoporosis for example? If, when you press, there is no pain, then there is no danger. If there is pain, reduce your pressure. Scared of pressing on the abdomen of someone who suffers from a hiatus hernia, same thing applies, no pain no danger. Pain = reduce pressure until your pressure is painless. There are still some contraindications that we should heed whether there is pain or not. The most important ones are when there are blood clots or risk of getting them, or the risk of a stroke, for example because of widespread atherosclerosis.

From what you may have read in previous chapters, one might get the impression that in any treatment, the person receiving Heisei Shiatsu can have deep pressure applied in that particular treatment. This is not the case.

Sometimes a person, and more commonly an area of the body of a particular patient, can – and should – receive light, superficial pressure. As I have pointed out before, a good shiatsu practitioner knows how to regulate their pressure and apply from the deepest (remember, never strong, hard or pointy but deep) to the lightest or more superficial pressure.

It is easy to know when to apply very superficial pressure, which is almost, but not quite, a static hold. It suffices to apply the no-pain principle. Pressure should never be painful mostly for two reasons, because pain makes muscles contract when we want them to relax, and because we don't believe pain leads to more effective treatments.

The clearest – and in my experience the most common – case for this, is when we encounter low back pain. In most instances of low back pain, I can apply deep pressure everywhere in the body except in the painful area where that would cause more pain. That area is already sore, and has usually been sore for some time, sometimes years. Manipulating a sore area should be done with the utmost care so as not to provoke any pain. In the worst cases, we need to avoid the area entirely.

What I personally do is, while giving shiatsu, to look for signs of any discomfort. If one sees the person grimacing or tensing up the body, it means we need to reduce the intensity of our pressure. I always ask patients to tell me if it hurts, but I have learnt the hard way that many of them do not wish to say it, and many others believe that pain is good, that it leads to a better treatment, so I think it is important to be alert to the signals emanating from the body.

There are more extreme cases than the lower back pain one. I have had cases when almost the whole body could not take anything but the lightest of pressure. As in most instances, these people can little by little get used to deeper pressure without feeling any pain, and not only they enjoy it, but realise how its effects are more profound.

I normally insist on learners being in relative good health when they are beginners. Learners have to exchange their practice with other learners and it is quite often difficult for beginners or inexperienced practitioners to know how to adjust their pressure or apply light pressure when necessary. At the beginning, one doesn't really know how to easily change the intensity of the pressure.

How to reduce intensity of pressure

There are several ways to apply light pressure, all of them difficult to illustrate with words. The only effective way I know of teaching this, is to have an assistant lie down and give instructions to the practitioner while the assistant gives feedback. What beginners find hard to believe is that I still use the weight of my body and the movement of my hips to apply very light pressure. It is done via a mixture of the position of the arms, the hands and most important, my intention.

The arms, as I have stated before, are levers through which I transmit pressure from my body weight. The more extended the arms are, the deeper the pressure is. To reduce the intensity, I bend my arms at the same time as my weight is going down towards the patient. As several things in a good shiatsu, it is a question of coordination. If I coordinate the movement of the body with the bending of the arms, the result is superficial pressure that causes no pain, even in areas or muscles which are sore.

How I position my hands and thumbs also has an effect on the intensity. Flatter hands and flatter thumbs are needed to reduce pressure.

Following the no-pain principle not only makes it easy to give a very fluid shiatsu with its dance-like sequence and treatment, it leads to the enjoyment of the session, the deep relaxation felt by patients and, above all, to more effective treatments and increased chances of musculoskeletal pain relief.

No-pain treatments are more effective because the body is a whole. Muscles, ligaments, tendons or joints do not exist or work in isolation. Muscles work together to perform functional activities.

The tightening or shortening of muscle fibres can cause muscle contractures reducing the flexibility of the muscle, and can cause joints to become painful. The shortening of a muscle leads to compensation in adjacent and distant muscles, which in turn means that what affects those adjacent and distant muscles also affects the shortened muscle. You don't necessarily need to work on a specific muscle to produce an effect on that muscle.

In other words, if you work deeply in the areas where you can, and superficially in the areas where you cannot go deeply because of painful muscles or joints, the effects are felt in the whole body, even in those areas where we have worked more superficially. There is no need for pain to combat pain.

In my opinion, intensity of pressure is also best reduced in some cases when there is no physical reason for it. If the patient is apprehensive or is afraid that our touch will cause pain, I think it is better to start with light pressure and increase it as the patient becomes more confident, as the next case history shows.

Case history: at the hospital

Not long ago I was working at the hospital where I treat cancer patients, and offered a treatment to a woman in her early fifties whom I will call Daisy. Daisy's case was a bit complicated from the point of view of integrative therapies in a hospital setting, because she had not had her scan yet, and the doctors believed the cancer had spread to certain areas but were not yet sure.

I explained to Daisy that due to these suspicions, the treatment would mainly consist of working on the legs and feet, ending with the head. When I mentioned this, she immediately curled up and moved her legs from within my reach.

She explained to me that she suffered from osteoarthritis in both legs and feet, and that she was scared of my "massage" being painful. I assured her that it wasn't going to be painful, but she was very reluctant to let me try. After about ten minutes of conversation, with me trying to convince her to give it a go, she acquiesced quite reluctantly, and told me not to touch her knees.

Because of her fear, I didn't want to start with the usual deep pressure I do, not because I thought it would hurt her or cause any pain, but because I needed to gain her trust.

She relaxed after a few minutes of my treatment giving me the thumbs up every time I was checking her face for any signs of pain. I did touch her knees and there was no reaction. Her face showed how she was enjoying the treatment more and more. When I reached the calves, I noticed they were quite tense, so I increased the pressure, always checking to see if she grimaced or tensed up her body which she never did. When I reached the feet, I began to apply my usual deep pressure to which she reacted by relaxing further. When I left, she thanked me and praised my massage.

Case history: a private client

I was working in a gym inside a big company in London for a number of years. The gym membership was exclusive for the employees who had a discount in all the activities. The first time one of my most regular clients came to see me, he could not take anything but the lightest of pressures in almost the whole of his body. The only area of his body where I could apply any type of deeper pressure were the feet. And that is what I did. Work on the feet quite a bit with deeper pressure, and work on the rest of the body with the lightest of pressures. I do not remember exactly, but I think it was about six or seven sessions before I could apply deep pressure all over the body. Sensitive people get used to deeper pressure with not too much effort on our part as therapists. It is simply a question of time.

Later, he asked me what I had found (diagnosed) treating him, and I told him about him not being able to have deep pressure at the beginning. His reply was: it was a difficult moment for me.

Speed revisited

Controlling one's speed of entering and exiting is one of the key elements to avoid pain. Apart from the already stated advisable feature of having the same speed to apply pressure – entering – as to withdraw it – exiting – some patients, sometimes because of their constitution, and other times because of their condition, require us to speed up or slow down our treatment speed. This is where our intuition and our experience come in very handy. They both guide us to the best possible treatment.

However, from the point of view of the no-pain principle, we should follow first and foremost the actual feedback from the patient. If in doubt, go more slowly, in fact, in the worst cases, when patients are weak or apprehensive go as slowly as possible. They will relax even more than what you expected.

When is it difficult to apply the no-pain principle?

Do you want to know when it is really, really hard to apply the no-pain principle in a treatment? When the patient insists that pain is good for you and that if there is no pain nothing is happening. Some patients insist on therapists applying the hardest possible pressure, they want those muscles to hurt, they believe that pain is the only measurement of successful treatments. It doesn't matter how much they have relaxed, if there is no pain, then they are not happy. It doesn't matter that their muscles feel looser after the treatment, there was no pain during the treatment and that is bad in their eyes.

Do you want to know why it is hard to apply the no-pain treatment in those cases? Because you spend a lot of energy explaining that you can achieve the aims of looser and more relaxed muscles without the pain, because you spend so much energy trying to convince them that the pleasure of painless treatments is effective when they have already made their mind up.

初心 (しょしん) Beginner's mind

No-pain is not only a guiding principle, it is also a great teacher. Every new person I treat is in reality a new case. I do not know how they are going to react, whether my shiatsu is going to be of great or little benefit to them, or even how to best approach their case whatever their constitution and condition is. A new concern, a new patient, requires new learning on my part. Many times I also need to look at someone I have treated before with new eyes, since their condition has changed. Of course my experience guides me, and the more experience I acquire, the more confident I feel. But my experience should not make me lose sight of the fact that this person is not any of the people I have treated before, and that not two organisms are exactly the same, and even that the same organism changes over time.

If we do not want to get stuck in our knowledge, if we want to continue learning, then the Zen principle of Shoshin (初心) or beginner's mind can help us.

This is a state of being in which we acknowledge that we do not know what comes next, we do not assume in what way the patient is going to react, our mind is open and we observe, we let ourselves be as sensitive and receptive as possible, and we really observe and act accordingly, we act according to what we perceive and not to what we think we should perceive. This state of being, this open-mindedness, will permit us to continuously acquire new knowledge about our shiatsu and thus help us in future, but above all, it leads us to a more empathetic understanding of the real person we are dealing with. This in turn results in the avoidance of disappointments, especially in challenging circumstances.

Which brings us back to what I have been talking about all along, the no-pain principle. Pain is elusive and changing. What is painful today might not be tomorrow and vice versa, although sometimes pain stays on the same spot for a long time. In a practical shiatsu situation, this means that I might suddenly encounter a painful spot when, for example, all the surrounding area is painless or the exact same spot was not painful before. If I approach my shiatsu with an open mind, without judging or asking myself why, if I approach the situation with the mind of a beginner, I should notice the pain by seeing their facial expression, and either reduce the pressure or slow down my rhythm or both. I do not ask myself why a spot is suddenly painful. I do not judge. I simply react. This has happened to me even with a whole body treatment, some people need a slower rhythm than others and vice versa, some people or situations require a quicker rhythm.

As the Japanese saying goes: "never forget the beginner's mind".

If you want to know how the no-pain principle can improve your shiatsu treatments, keep on reading, a few of the case histories might surprise you.

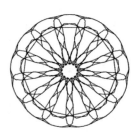

Chapter 10

Shiatsu and the relaxation response

Stress

Life requires all organisms to adapt and resist stress, a process in which our vital organs and functions take part. If we are to survive, our bodies need to adapt all the time to the changing internal and external environment. As part of this adaptation, there are internal processes in our bodies that regulate our physiological state so that the parameters are balanced. This is what is known as homeostasis. It is mostly through the nervous system that the body maintains homeostasis. This has been speculated as being one of the reasons for the health benefits of shiatsu which is believed to balance the nervous system.

We are all affected by stress, which can have an impact in every aspect of our lives. According to the World Health Organization (WHO), everyone experiences stress to some degree, since our body is designed to react to stress. But the way an individual responds to stress, or how long they are under stressful circumstances, makes a big difference to their wellbeing. Stress affects our body and our brains. Some stress is many times necessary to cope with daily, unexpected or dangerous situations because it allows us to adjust. It is life-saving when we encounter a dangerous situation to which the reaction is fight or flight. Our health and even our longevity are affected by our response to stress.

From a physiological point of view, stress can directly have a negative impact on the autonomic and neuroendocrine systems and it can also lead to behavioural changes that affect negatively on our health.

When we are exposed to repeated or prolonged stressful situations, our bodies lose the ability to properly respond to those situations.

If this happens, problems arise because long-term stress without adequate relaxation becomes chronic, which in turn may lead to a series of health issues. Acute stress, when we experience a short reaction to a challenging or stressful situation, increases our blood pressure, our heart and breathing rate and the temperature of our body rises. These reactions disappear after a while and go back to normal.

Chronic stress, on the other hand, usually provokes a continued response that leads to body deterioration. It can affect the immune system, the heart, the lungs, the digestive system, our sexual function, it usually leads to muscular problems and can even increase sugar and cholesterol levels, as well as have a deleterious effect on the menstrual cycle. In the case of muscular reactions to stress, the muscles tighten and find it increasingly hard to relax. Many chronic pains and aches including tension headaches can be related to the body's acquired inability to relax the muscles.

The relaxation response

The relaxation response is a physical and chemical reaction from our bodies which is the opposite of how our bodies react under stress, the opposite of the fight-or-flight response. Under the relaxation response our bodies return to normal and the autonomic nervous system is no longer in overdrive, thus allowing our bodily functions to resume their tasks without damaging our health. There are different types of practices that help bring about this response.

According to scientists, these practices help lower blood pressure and heart rate with the ensuing health benefits that this leads to, including the prevention of many adverse conditions such as hypertension, arthritis or insomnia. The relaxation response releases hormones that make us feel better, the so-called feel-good chemicals.

Usually, the main aim of shiatsu is not relaxation. Shiatsu is above all a therapeutic technique that aims to improve the health of those who receive it. One of the aims of shiatsu, from a Western physiology point of view, is to balance the autonomic nervous system, to achieve balance between the sympathetic and parasympathetic systems so that it relaxes us when we are tense or anxious, and it gives us energy when we feel lethargic or tired.

As explained before, these two states are not mutually exclusive, feeling less tired makes us more relaxed, not less. There are studies in Japan about the balancing effects of shiatsu on the autonomic nervous system. Please see the references at the end of the book.

What is clear is that most people who come for a session are to a higher or lower degree stressed and that shiatsu makes the receiver reach a profound relaxation state.

Why depth of pressure matters: a physiological point of view

As explained in the chapter about touch and science, the mechanoreceptors found within joint capsular tissues, ligaments, tendons, muscle, and skin have an important role to play in the physiological response of our bodies to tactile feedback from the skin and the skeletal system. The mechanoreceptors detect and react to touch, pressure, stretch, movement and vibration, and are involved in the inhibition of nociceptors, the nerve cell endings that transmit pain impulses, which is one of the reasons why the stimulation of mechanoreceptors leads to pain reduction and relief.

When connective tissue, which provides cohesion and internal support to bone, ligaments, tendons and surrounds muscles, is in a normal state, mechanoreceptors react and respond, while when its environment is abnormal, the nociceptors react causing pain.

Comparing shallow or medium-depth pressure to deep pressure, I think it is obvious that the first two would not reach or stimulate those mechanoreceptors found at the subcutaneous level to the same extent as deeper pressure would, thus producing a lower relaxation response and making the inhibition of pain less likely[14]. I believe – and I have observed – that deep pressure leads to a more relaxed state and, if on top of that, deep pressure is painless, it is more enjoyable and much more effective at reducing pain and providing relief for a longer period of time, since it does not stimulate the nociceptors at all.

When deep pressure is painful, even if it is only slightly, although the effect is felt by the body as helping with its pain, it cannot be as effective since it is also transmitting pain signals to the brain, signals that help inhibit to a certain extent what the mechanoreceptors perceive and transmit. Anything that stimulates the nociceptors is best avoided since it may affect negatively the outcome of the treatment.

Anxiety or let' s revisit speed again

When we encounter a patient who is feeling anxious for whatever reason that may be, we need to adapt our treatment and our attitude towards that person. Anxiety in shiatsu treatments is noticed mostly for how talkative the person is.

---

[14] Although it is a study on massage and weight gain for preterm infants, I think it is interesting to note the different effects from one type of pressure to the other. Field, T., Diego, M.A., Hernandez-Reif, M., Deeds, O. and Figuereido, B., 2006. Moderate versus light pressure massage therapy leads to greater weight gain in preterm infants. *Infant Behavior and Development*, 29(4), pp.574-578.

Sometimes it is as if they cannot help themselves and their time with us as therapists is like an escape valve. We should of course respect that and let them talk and reply if they expect us to do so. Sometimes, they themselves acknowledge their anxiety, as happened to me once when working with a cancer patient. She was talkative throughout the whole session, and told me of how she felt anxious about her diagnosis.

To calm these patients down, one has to adjust the speed and, in my experience, the most calming effect can be obtained by starting with a relatively quick speed and, when we feel the person is ready, we *gradually* slow it down. As always, we should not overdo it. Too quick a pressure would make them more anxious as it would a slow pace.

It is not a question of how fast can one apply shiatsu, but what speed that person needs at that particular moment. All I can say is that it has worked for me in the majority of cases.

Case history: shiatsu and relaxation

When I was a beginning student I always tried to find people who would be willing to receive shiatsu so that I could practise. I had a classmate who lived near me and many times we practised together. The first time we practised together was at my home on two persons, one a friend of mine and the other one, a friend of my friend. They had never even heard of shiatsu and they both came with towels because they thought of classical massage with oil. After we had finished our practice, they both talked to us about their experience. First, they expressed surprise at how relaxing the treatment was. They mentioned how, when lying down, they both thought it was not going to be as relaxing as classical massage because there was no kneading of muscles, which is what they related to relaxation, so they were surprised when they felt so nicely calm when we had only applied stationary pressure.

The vast majority of the patients I have treated and who give me feedback, describe the aftereffect as so relaxing that they feel they are floating in the air, or as if they were in a cloud.

Heisei Shiatsu as movement meditation: another case history

As I said in the prologue, I started working with shiatsu above a hairdresser's. The reception was the same for both businesses and patients had to pay at the end of my treatments downstairs, which was also where the waiting area was. I usually accompanied my patients downstairs to check if I had a new patient waiting, so I saw the receptionist and the hairdressers if they happened to be free at that moment. They didn't know much about shiatsu but seemed to like what they saw, which was very relaxed faces coming down. Once, when I came down, and the patient had already left, they saw how relaxed I was and asked me, with their typical sense of humour, have you been giving or receiving shiatsu?

Giving shiatsu can be very relaxing too. After all these years, I still count internally to myself, so that I can follow a steady rhythm. I consider this steady rhythm and the rocking of my body that comes with it as moving meditation. My concentration on what I am doing does the rest and I usually feel more relaxed after giving shiatsu.

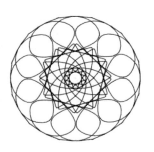

Chapter 11
Abdominal Shiatsu

The benefits

No, I am not talking about the palpation of the abdomen in order to diagnose. Hara diagnosis, as it is called, has been extensively explained in books, manuals and videos. I am talking about something else, about applying pressure on the abdomen, something that many shiatsu therapists and teachers seem to forego. Some apply pressure, but seem to be scared of deep pressure on the abdomen, as if it could not be done, others use a Tui Na technique of applying pressure with the four fingers extended, which means you cannot use the weight of your body to apply pressure because you would hurt your fingers, yet others apply pressure with the edge of the hand which is quite painful and can only result in shallow pressure, and the majority simply do without. But abdominal shiatsu, when done properly, is very beneficial.

Deep, slow, abdominal shiatsu aids systemic and pulmonary circulation, nourishes body cells, helps fight diseases and maintain homeostasis. It makes our breathing deeper because it works directly on the diaphragm and it can help with many types of back and sciatica pain since it reaches and affects the rectus abdominis muscle directly, and although the iliopsoas muscle is a more profound muscle, we can also reach it. If the rectus abdominis and iliopsoas are tight or contracted, the low back suffers. The contracture in the iliopsoas pulls the vertebrae causing excessive lordosis (low-back curvature) and an excessive tilted pelvis.

The rectus abdominis is an important spine stabiliser whose tension can lead to mid and lower back pain. A study carried out in Japan showed that abdominal shiatsu had a beneficial effect in adjusting the sacral tilt[15].

The same researchers believe that abdominal shiatsu helps regulate the autonomic nervous system with a decrease in heart and blood pressure rates. By pressing on the abdomen we can stimulate gastrointestinal mobility or peristalsis, and thus improve digestion. From a shiatsu perspective, it also allows us to diagnose at the same time we are applying our shiatsu. We can combine Oriental and Western diagnosis, Oriental diagnosis of organs/meridians, of kyo and jitsu, and Western diagnosis of the state of the muscles we are in contact with. We can also assess if there are any particular painful points and work to reduce the pain. Many of these points only feel tender to the touch and cannot be evaluated otherwise.

The no-pain principle revisited: our speed again

In Heisei Shiatsu, we still apply the no-pain principle when working on the abdomen. It is probably the most delicate area of the body in this respect, probably because giving access to so many of our internal organs makes us feel vulnerable. This is clearly seen in the reaction some people have when we press on the abdomen. They suddenly want to control our speed, they tense up the abdominal muscles and try to push up our thumbs or palms. As in any other area of the body, when we find apprehension, we should decrease the intensity of our pressure and our speed and rhythm. With time, patients will begin to trust us and let us apply the deep pressure on the abdomen which is so beneficial.

---

[15] See references section

For a patient to be able to receive deep pressure in the abdomen, there are three basic conditions without which only the most superficial of pressures can be applied. The first condition is the one already mentioned, the patient needs to let go and trust the therapist.

The second condition comes from both the therapist and the patient being relaxed, but much more so from the attitude and stance of the therapist. The therapist needs to be very relaxed. Any tension on the part of the therapist affects any part of the body they are working on, but this effect is multiplied in the case of the abdomen. Relaxed shoulders, arms, hands and the therapist's own abdomen are essential to be able to apply deep pressure in this case. The third condition is to have a slow speed and rhythm when pressing the abdomen.

Unless we press slowly, both in entering and exiting and in our rhythm, pressure can only be very superficial. There is something very special when one feels the moment the patient lets go and accepts our pressure on their abdomen. It is as if a new type of connection is established between therapist and patient. But remember, it might take quite a while before they become so accepting but the result is worth the wait.

Abdominal shiatsu to aid digestion

Shiatsu on the abdomen can help with digestive problems. When working on the abdomen, we usually press in a clockwise direction, that is to say, in the same direction digestion takes place in the large intestine.

Peristalsis is the involuntary contraction and relaxation of muscles that move food through the digestive tract, and these movements begin in the mouth and end in the anus. By applying pressure in the abdomen in a clockwise direction, we help the movement of the food in that particular section of the digestive tract. We try to replicate the flow of our digestive system.

This is also the reason why we usually finish our abdominal shiatsu by pressing on the points of the sigmoid colon, which is where we can affect the last movement of the digestive process.

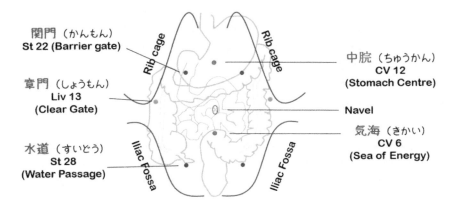

関門 （かんもん）
St 22 (Barrier gate)

章門 （しょうもん）
Liv 13
(Clear Gate)

水道 （すいどう）
St 28
(Water Passage)

中脘 （ちゅうかん）
CV 12
(Stomach Centre)

Navel

気海 （きかい）
CV 6
(Sea of Energy)

Some of the meridian points on the abdomen
pressed in Heisei Shiatsu

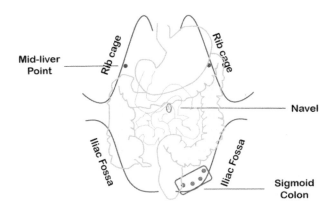

Mid-liver
Point

Navel

Sigmoid
Colon

Some points outside meridians on the abdomen

Sometimes, when we are treating chronic constipation, the abdomen or our patient is so hard that our pressure can be anything but deep and it can only have a very limited effect.

We can then make use of other type of tools we have at our disposal, tools that are obviously also available when treating less serious cases of digestive disorders. The body has autonomic reflexes that control many of the activities of our internal organs. Some of these have been mapped out by Western physiology and others that have been in use for a long time in Traditional Chinese and Japanese Medicine. Quite a few of them, but not all, coincide in both systems.

The vagus nerve plays a big role in the speed of digestion. At the same time, it transmits signals from your gut to your brain. As such, it might come as no surprise that stimulating the vagus nerve can help with a number of digestion-related illnesses, including inflammatory bowel disease. The vagus nerve is responsible for the release of neurotransmitters that increase the production of gastric acid, which is essential for our digestion and to protect the stomach from bacteria and viruses. An overactive or underactive vagus nerve can lead to the hypersecretion or hyposecretion of gastric acid with all the resulting problems that this entails.

Shiatsu can stimulate the vagus nerve as it passes through the anterior neck, which coincides with three of the stomach points of the Stomach Meridian in TCM.

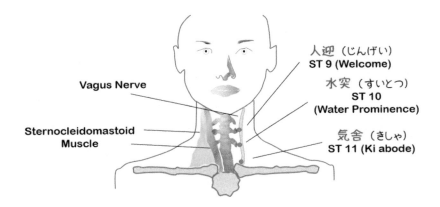

Another point we usually press in order to help with any type of digestive problem is Stomach 36. This point is called Sanri in Japanese and it has a special place in Traditional Japanese Medicine. There are four Sanri points on the body, two on the legs and two on the arms. These points have been used traditionally in Japan to provide energy to the body. According to tradition, moxa was applied at the sanri spot to help the person run fast. It was said that it was the habit of the early Japanese to have moxa applied at the point Sanri before a trip to help them walk further than otherwise they would have been capable of.

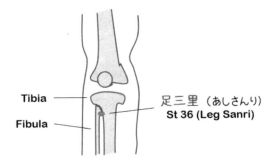

One of the four sanri points on the body used to increase energy, the leg sanri can also be used to help with digestive problems.

Natural versus forced breathing

Breathing exercises are very beneficial for our health and, as every therapist does, I sometimes use them to teach patients to breathe more deeply. Generally speaking, that is not my goal. My goal is to promote deeper breathing in a natural way, so that patients do not need to think about breathing in order to breathe as deeply as possible without paying any attention. My goal is for patients to breathe deeply without thinking about it, and if possible, not only during the shiatsu sessions, but also in their daily life, which is probably much more difficult.

I have been asked a few times whether I ask patients to breathe in before I press and then breathe out while I am pressing on a particular point. The reply is no, I don't do that, *except* in a few occasions. I tend to ask them to pay attention to their breathing only when I realise how much in control they need to be. Some patients cannot really let go and trust me with their breathing, so, as I have said before, some of them tense up the abdominal muscles, and others *force* their breathing to be deep. In these cases, I do ask them to follow the rhythm of my pressure when breathing in and out.

I do not claim that because you receive regular abdominal shiatsu, or because you do breathing exercises, your breathing will always be deep and natural. Unfortunately, stressful situations and other factors of our daily lives make our breathing shallower and faster. In these type of situations, we don't even realise that this is happening, we usually notice it afterwards, when we try to relax. But, as breathing exercises help us breathe more deeply naturally, so does receiving abdominal shiatsu.

Abdominal shiatsu applies pressure directly on the diaphragm, which is the major muscle of respiration. The fact that our pressure is rhythmic also helps the diaphragm to find a slow natural relaxed rhythm as well as aiding in the expansion and contraction of the thoracic cavity.

From my own experience, I believe we can use shiatsu on the abdomen to calm people down *as long as we don't start on the abdomen*. This is better understood from the information given about the treatment of anxiety in the previous chapter. One has to be wary of wanting to calm down patients too quickly.

In the worst cases, in those patients who have suffered or may suffer panic attacks, caution is even more essential. If we try to relax them too quickly, they might have the opposite reaction. Slowly does it, or as the Japanese would say 急がば回れ.

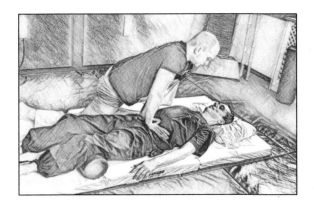

When both the patient and the therapist are relaxed abdominal shiatsu can be very profound.

Chapter 12

Improvement of health conditions is not all or nothing, it can be gradual

I find it odd, to say the least, that generally speaking, complementary therapies are usually judged more harshly than conventional medicine or than the effects of pharmaceutical drugs.

Let me illustrate with an example. If someone suffers, let's say, from regular headaches, something like once a week, they might take a drug prescribed by a doctor or from the chemist's. Let's assume what I believe is a very plausible scenario. The drug reduces the headache intensity by 70%, but the person needs to take it regularly, usually as regularly as the advent of their headaches, so in our hypothetical case, once a week.

Now let's say that this person goes to a complementary therapist, a massage therapist or an osteopath or a shiatsu therapist. Let's imagine that in the first session the pain is only reduced 40%, but that, after a few sessions, the reduction in pain reaches 60%, but more importantly, the frequency is much reduced and the person only suffers from headaches every fortnight, a reduction of 50% in frequency.

For some reason, many publications, and many patients too, would consider the second case a failure. They ask of complementary therapies what they do not ask of conventional medicine, they ask for 100% improvement or they consider it a failure, although, in my eyes, the second case would be more of a success than the first case.

Case history: when you don't give a therapy a chance

I once treated a woman whom I will call Sophie. Sophie was in her mid-thirties, suffered from terrible migraines, and wanted to try a different approach from the prescription drugs she was taking.

She came to see me, and after the shiatsu treatment we had a relatively long chat. She told me how many therapists she had seen for this problem and I was astonished. I do not remember how many therapists she had seen, but it was in excess of five. She had seen two acupuncturists, an osteopath a chiropractor, a massage therapist and others I don't remember. So what is the catch? She had seen all of them only once and she told me how it hadn't worked.

Astonished is probably an understatement. What I told her was to stick to one – not me, anyone – for a bit longer, that she couldn't expect to be relieved of such a problem in one session, no matter what technique was used. Moreover, if she had the session on a day in which she didn't suffer from the migraine, it would be difficult to appreciate its effects, so perhaps she should concentrate more on measuring frequency. As you can imagine, I never saw her again, and from the expression on her face, I doubt very much that she paid any attention to my recommendation.

Why, if by taking the prescription drugs once your migraines do not disappear you don't consider it a failure, but, having a complementary therapies treatment once you do? I have no answers, it is a mystery to me.

Treating musculoskeletal problems

The general public at large is so used to think of shiatsu as something that works on meridians and energy that they forget that shiatsu has an effect – and an important one at that – on nerves and muscles too. Shiatsu relaxes contracted muscles and triggers the stretch reflex helping those muscles become more supple.

With patients that come to see me with musculoskeletal problems, which is probably the most common cause for them to seek my help, there is something I almost invariably do. To "prove" that the treatment is working, if they come let's say with neck stiffness, I ask them to move the neck to the side with both movements, neck rotation and lateral flexion (side-bending) in front of a mirror, *and stop the movement as soon as they feel any pain or discomfort*. After the treatment, I ask them to perform the same movements and tell me if the movement can go further *without pain or discomfort*.

It is my way of showing them that the treatment is working. The fact that they see their movements in a mirror helps them compare the movements before and after treatments and in many occasions the movement has improved.

Treatment 1. Low back pain

How do I avoid causing any pain when treating low back pain? Before I explain how I do it, I need to repeat something. The body is a whole, muscles, ligaments and tendons do not act in isolation and shiatsu is a holistic treatment. So, if I have the time, I treat most of the body, but follow a few basic rules.

As one can imagine, these are not hard-and-fast rules, they are simply basic rules that one can more or less follow depending on the actual person we are treating and their condition.

The main rule I follow is the no-pain principle. This extends to the position of the patient. They need to be in a comfortable position which does not make the pain worse and from which they can stand up without causing any more pain. In the worst cases, this implies working with people sitting down and not using the couch. In other cases, they need to lie on their side.

Please note that these positions are temporary. As the patient improves, they can then go on to a position that allows us to work in more areas and which are more comfortable for us. Whether they can lie on the couch or not, I do not start by working on the lower back. This is the area that hurts and I usually leave it till the end. What I most certainly do, is work a lot on the hamstrings. As most specialists in this field know, tight hamstring muscles increases stress on the low back and can lead to sciatic nerve root pressure. Relaxing and lengthening hamstrings reduces the strain on the spine. Pressing on the calf muscles with the aim of decontracting them is another part of the treatment since tight calf muscles increase the pull on the lower back when walking. I also work on the ilipsoas muscle by pressing on the abdomen. One day I was working on the abdomen of a woman with chronic back pain who was surprised because the pressure on the abdomen was relieving her back pain. I explained to her about the iliopsoas muscle and its relation with back pain and gave her some stretching exercises for this muscle.

And finally, as I have previously explained, I then treat the painful area with light pressure so as not to cause any pain which, in my opinion, makes the treatment nicer and more effective since pain only makes muscles contract. This treatment has to be completed by working on the sacrum, especially in cases of sciatica pain.

What about points for low back pain? First a warning that you may remember from the prologue. I think that one should be cautious when talking about specific points on the body for something. Although these can help, they are not a panacea that you can simply press and all the pain dissolves. As explained many times, shiatsu is a holistic treatment.

But the points do help. We should press these points from between one and two minutes. For back pain, we can press the acupuncture point Gallbladder 20 (風池 in Japanese). But beware, I said *help*, not that pressing on that point is a magical process that solves the issue. If it was that easy I'd be a millionaire by now.

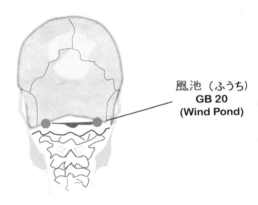

風池 (ふうち)
GB 20
(Wind Pond)

Gallbladder 20. At the base of the skull,
lateral to the tendons of the trapezius muscle
風池 (ふうち) wind pond

To know more about back pain from a Traditional Chinese Medicine (TCM) point of view, please see the video in the references section.

Treatment 2. Neck stiffness

As always, I follow the no-pain principle. In case of neck stiffness, the massage table is a very useful tool indeed, since this is one of the cases when having the neck to one side even for short periods of time would make the stiffness and pain worse. If we do not have access to a massage table with a face hole or face cushion extension, or if we prefer to work on the futon, then part of the treatment should be done with the person lying on their side, but never face down.

Even on the massage table with the face in the middle, I try to make the time they lie on their stomach as short as possible. This is done mostly to work on the trapezius and rhomboid muscles which, in my experience, and that of many others, helps with any type of neck problems.

The other major area to relieve stiffness or pain in the neck are the arms. Relaxing the muscles of the arms provides relief to the shoulders and the neck. We should add shoulder rotations to our treatment. Rotating the shoulders helps the whole neck area relax. As for points, I usually press Gallbladder 21 (肩井 in Japanese) for about two to three minutes.

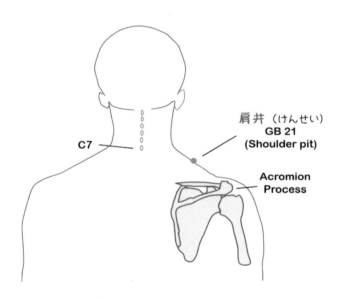

Gallbladder 21 肩井 (けんせい shoulder pit or shoulder well). In Namikoshi shiatsu, this point is called the suprascapular point. The point is in the shoulder cavity which is as deep as a well.
At the highest point of the shoulder, midway between the acromion and spinous process of C7

Chapter 13

Working on the massage table is the same

How to adapt shiatsu to any situation

Shiatsu in Japan: practicality

Curiously, in Japan, it is more common to receive shiatsu on a table/couch than on a futon. This is mostly attributed by practitioners to the fact that kneeling on futons for lengthy periods of time can damage the knees. But I think there are other clear advantages to working on the couch (depending on type of couch), and at least one very distinct advantage of learning to give shiatsu on the couch, even if later one prefers the futon (which has other advantages). I said curiously, because Japanese people are more used than Westerners to kneeling, so, if anything, to give shiatsu, they would need the couch less than Westerners, but they use it more.

From the point of view of the receiver, one of the most important advantages of the table/couch is that they can lie face down with the head in the middle, something that is important when you have neck or back problems. It is of course imperative that patients who find it difficult to lie down on the floor or to get up because of health issues, or because of their age, are treated on a couch. It would be ridiculous to tell someone who finds it difficult and painful to go up or down the stairs to lie down at floor level. From the point of view of the practitioner, it makes working on the shoulders easier, especially on the side the head would be turned to on a futon or mattress, and it allows for faster movements when changing position.

It makes certain stretches easier to perform and, as stated before, it helps in cases where practitioners have knee problems. It also makes it easier to do articular rotations, especially, but not exclusively, ankle and toe rotations.

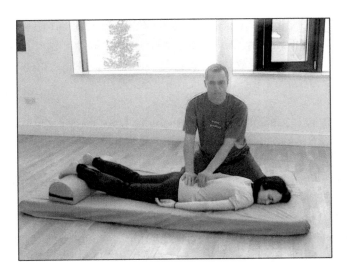

On the futon, the head needs to be turned to one side

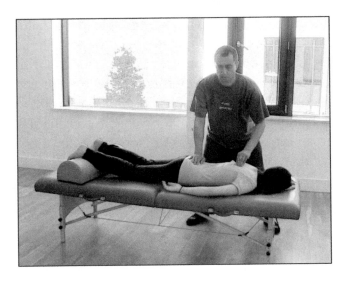

The couch has a face hole that allows patients
to have the head in the middle and breathe freely

As in massage, shiatsu couches are better suited for practitioners if they are adjusted to their height. But couches need to go lower for shiatsu than for massage, to permit the full movement of the hips and the complete use of gravity when leaning towards the patient – remember that the whole weight of the body is better than half the weight. The usual height of normal massage couches would mean that the movement of the body would be restricted, making it impossible to apply a deep pressure and making it harder for the practitioner's back.

Personally, I see other advantages to have trained in working on the couch. It has taught me the flexibility of shiatsu treatments which can be adapted to most situations, and how shiatsu can be given almost anywhere. Working on inpatients in hospital beds has been made much easier for me thanks to my training; I can even reach areas other therapists do not usually work on when those patients have mobility problems and find it difficult or painful to change their position. I never ask patients to change their position. In fact, it is painful for me seeing their efforts to "facilitate" my work by moving when this is so painful for them. I always have to tell them that they don't need to do anything, it is me who adapts to their situation. But not only that, it has also facilitated my work with patients in wheelchairs, and even working with people when all I had was a chair. For example, I have treated people who have come to me with a broken arm in a plaster cast when I was working with the special massage chair. I think it is obvious I couldn't ask them to lean on the special chair, so I asked them to sit down on a normal chair and worked on their neck, and upper shoulders.

Giving shiatsu on a special chair in a park in London

Gravity revisited

In all cases, whether I work on a futon, on a couch, with the patient in bed or in a wheelchair or with someone sitting in a sofa, I never forget to use my body weight as the tool to apply pressure. It does not matter what my position is in relation to the patient, I always let gravity help me. My body leans forward and transmits pressure through my arms and hands. I sometimes have to work on my knees, it does not change anything, my hips move forward with the rest of the body even if the distance covered is shorter than the distance covered when working on a futon or couch. The movement might be shorter because of my position, but nonetheless there is always some movement brought about by me letting go of my body and letting gravity do the rest of the work. The basic principle of not using one's own strength, but letting gravity work for us is, in my opinion, essential if we want our shiatsu to be painless and acquire the depth adequate for the person we are working on.

As I said before, the couch is not different from the futon, it still requires the use of our body weight, and the positions are relatively similar to the ones I use on the futon. These positions have simply been adapted slightly.

Case history: working with a patient in a wheelchair

I treated quite a few times a patient who had lung cancer and whom I shall call Will. Because of his illness, Will had lost the ability to walk, and had to rely on a wheelchair when he wanted to move around the hospital. He still had to stay in the hospital because he was not deemed suitable to be discharged. After a few shiatsu sessions with me that took place while he was in his bed, one day, I found him in his wheelchair. I asked him if he wanted a shiatsu session, but, on that occasion, he seemed very reluctant to go ahead. It took me about 3 minutes of talking to him to realise that he expected me to ask him to move to his bed to receive shiatsu, which was obviously a burden for him. I assured him that he could have the shiatsu treatment he so much loved in his wheelchair. With this assurance, he accepted, and not only did he enjoy my treatment, but he never hesitated again, not even for a second.

Which brings us to the why. Why a therapy that is so versatile, that patients do not have to move when they can't or they don't feel like it in order to receive it, a therapy that can reach parts of the body that provide relief from pain even in difficult circumstances, is, in so, so many places, rejected as something not acceptable.

I can guess, although I cannot be 100% sure, but please hear me out, read my story in the next two chapters.

Chapter 14

Thank God for small mercies

One of my current roles

As you will discover in the next chapter, when I give an account of my long journey dealing with hospitals, charities and institutions, the strange beliefs and misconceptions about shiatsu are abundant, and changing the mind of those who have held those beliefs for so long is an arduous and thankless task. But one should be grateful for small mercies, and, if I have been able to change the mind of just a handful of people, then I guess it has been worth it.

At the time of writing I am volunteering for a charity that provides complementary and integrative therapies for patients with all types of disabilities including unseen disabilities. I appear to have changed – at least in part – the perspective on shiatsu of those who run the charity. Apart from changing the view that shiatsu is a very painful therapy – something they really believed because of their past experiences – I also had to change a few other misconceptions. I would say that changing the part of painful shiatsu treatments has been the easiest. First by giving treatments to the staff and then when they went on to ask patients how they felt during and after my treatments. We are conducting some research in this sense and the results are given in the next chapter.

But shiatsu being painful is not the only misconception I have heard many a time as the next anecdote illustrates. Once, I saw advertised a room to rent with a couch for complementary therapies inside a conservatoire in South London. The room was and is used for sports massage, acupuncture and craniosacral therapy.

I thought that it would be a good place to rent the room and show that shiatsu can help improve the health of performing artists, so I phoned the person in charge. When I mentioned the word shiatsu I almost felt her flinching on the other side of the line when she told me that shiatsu might not be appropriate because I would have to take the massage couch out of the room. When I said I normally did my shiatsu treatments on a massage couch, she became very agitated and told me that she knew everything about shiatsu before cutting me short. Strange, when I was going to pay the same as the others for using the room, but there you go.

So, although unrelated to that incident in the conservatoire, in my current role, I had to clarify a few written statements about shiatsu, which incidentally, had been written by past shiatsu therapists. That it "subtly works internally on the body". I don't think there is anything subtle about the effects of shiatsu. Many people describe the feeling as one of floating, of not wanting to get up, of being finally able to sleep and a sense of profound relaxation. I would call that a deep effect. That "the practitioner will gently touch your abdominal area to understand your body's energy levels". This is what therapists do in what is arguably the best-known shiatsu style, Zen (or Masunaga) Shiatsu, but it ignores completely the official shiatsu of Japan and other less well-known styles.
I do not think one should define *all* of shiatsu by one's particular style, although I believe this is not done on purpose but out of ignorance.

But the biggest – and most challenging – myth-busting exercise comes from contraindications and precautions. That is truly a shock for those of us who have worked with so many different conditions and patients.

That shiatsu should not be used in cases of cancer – which I do every week – epilepsy, which might be understandable in the case of drug-resistant (or uncontrolled) epilepsy.

But drug-resistant epilepsy is the rarer of the two. But there is one that for me is the strangest of all, the one I have read so many times.

The strange case of shiatsu and osteoporosis

Shiatsu contraindicated for osteoporosis? Where did that come from? Who spread such a ridiculous idea? I had never heard it until I moved to London, and I had already treated patients with osteoporosis. But more importantly, I remember the first time some colleagues of mine and I went to an Osteogenesis Imperfecta conference. Osteogenesis Imperfecta, also called brittle bone disease, is a rare genetic disorder that results in weak and fragile bones with bones that fracture easily, often with no obvious cause or trauma to the bone. Two other teachers and I attended the first time and gave shiatsu to those affected by this condition. In subsequent occasions we brought along any student who had finished the 2nd year and who wanted to come. In one occasion, there must have been about twelve of us. In every single instance we gave shiatsu to adults and children affected by this condition. We never told the students what to do or the need to adjust their treatment for the simple reason we trusted their pressure. We must have gone to these conferences about 5 or 6 times and not once we produced any fractures or bruises.

This I why I find it baffling to read or hear that osteoporosis is a contraindication in shiatsu. Obviously, the bones of those who suffer from brittle bone disease are much more fragile than those with osteoporosis. Whoever started that rumour must have either experienced a very hard, unprofessional shiatsu or be themselves a therapist with a strong, sharp, pointy pressure without any concept of how to soften their treatments, and I have to repeat it once more, in case it is not yet clear. To soften. Not to make their pressure less deep, not to apply light pressure. Deep pressure can be soft and enjoyable and safe.

Case history: I thought you were going to rip me apart

A woman with mild osteoporosis was one of my patients in this role. She came to see me because she suffered from piriformis syndrome. As part of the ongoing research project into how painful treatments are, the first time she came to see me, I asked her at the end of the session how painful the treatment had been on a scale of 0 to 10. She said that the treatment had not been painful at all and that she was surprised. This was the first time she had received shiatsu and she had read about it on the internet. From what she had read, she thought – as she put it – that I was going to rip her apart.

Chapter 15

Have I finally discovered why?

"It is easier to catch a liar
than to catch a one-legged man"
Spanish proverb

A mystifying shiatsu story

This is a story. Not a fairy story with a happy ending, but not a drama either. Just a real story. It is the story of the multiple times I have encountered rejections when applying, mostly for voluntary work, but sometimes for paid work, in hospitals and hospices in the UK. I was rejected because I used a very dreadful, spooky, scary word: shiatsu. Yes, you read that right. Shiatsu is a frightful, dirty word among many complementary therapists. No, not among doctors or nurses, oh no! The doctors and nurses and physiotherapists accept it and appreciate it. Shiatsu is a frightful word among the therapists and managers who run the complementary therapies departments in those hospitals and hospices. The last rejection was in February 2023.

Shiatsu, something apparently so scary and harmful and damaging that is not deemed appropriate by complementary therapist managers – except in a minority of cases. It is not considered appropriate even by shiatsu therapists who, although they are the ones in charge, refuse to introduce shiatsu to hospital and clinic services. I know of at least two in the UK. End of. They refuse to introduce it and they refuse to talk about it.

When you work with hospitalised patients, shiatsu has some very practical advantages. We work over the clothes, so the patients do not need to remove any item of clothing or part of it, except maybe for observation purposes. They do not even need to remove the socks when we work on the feet, which is very convenient for them if they are cold for instance. I do not even need them to remove their bed covers since I can work over these perfectly well. Shiatsu does not use creams or oils, so if the patient has already had a shower – if they can do it by themselves – or have been cleaned if they can't, there is no need to remove the cream or clean any areas I have worked on; the time of treatment according to their hospital routine is irrelevant. I can go at any time. Shiatsu can be applied on any part of the body, hands, feet, the back, the head, the face, the neck, the legs, etc., for as long as you need to. This makes shiatsu so versatile and useful that it can be applied in almost any situation in which we find patients.

For example, I can work on the trapezius muscle and the rhomboid muscles between the shoulder blades and the spine, and on the spinal nerves of that area (T-1 to T-5) *when the patient is lying on their back*. This last bit is extremely important to understand the versatility of shiatsu. I do not need to ask the patient to move their position, they don't need to lie on their side or face down for me to bring relief to an area that accumulates a lot of tension. I can introduce the fingers between the bed and their body and work on those areas and still use my body weight.

Shiatsu has become even more practical in hospital settings since the advent of covid-19. During the worst part of the pandemic, the integrated and complementary therapies services were closed down. When the service resumed, therapists were required to wear a plastic apron and gloves to treat patients. Shiatsu does not use sliding movements, so the use of gloves does not affect the quality of my pressure at all, nor does it make it any different for the patient.

I think that many therapists and integrative therapies services in hospitals resort to only hand and/or foot massage for the reasons I have explained before, the need to remove clothes to work on certain areas, the need for cleaning the oil or cream afterwards, or the fact that patients cannot easily change their position in bed. We, shiatsu therapists, still need to know the condition of the patient, same as the other therapists of course, so as to avoid contraindicated areas. This is why we have consultation forms and we get notes from the nurses.

But no more explanations. Now the story proper. Before moving to London, I had been a volunteer at a paediatric hospital in Spain for six years, working mostly in the dialysis section, although I also briefly gave shiatsu to the children in the paediatric ICU and in transplants. We went to the hospital three times a week and gave the children shiatsu for about half an hour before they were connected to the machines, although occasionally they arrived late, and the shiatsu treatment took place while they were already connected. The nurses, one summer, carried out an informal study of the benefits of shiatsu for these children who, for the most part, had been born with defective kidneys, and who needed to have their blood cleansed three times a week by being connected to the dialysis machines for about three to four hours each time. The replies from the patients was the same in almost every case. If they had had a shiatsu treatment before dialysis, they got fewer headaches and the sudden drops in blood pressure were not as abrupt, were more gradual, and although the dizziness was still there, it was much reduced.

With this experience in hand, I naïvely arrived in London, thinking that hospitals in the UK would be very happy to let me volunteer, and that shiatsu treatments would be considered one of the best practical solutions to offer treatments to hospitalised or bedridden patients.

Was I naïve! The complete opposite is the case. Shiatsu is a bad, scary word, a word that, in the setting of hospitals, makes these complementary therapists tense up as soon as you mention it, as if you had mentioned the devil himself.

Shiatsu is a therapy which is rejected by the vast majority of the integrated and complementary services in hospitals in the UK. Very few accept it, when all of them accept massage and reflexology, and, increasingly, reiki. I have been working with cancer patients in a hospital in London for over 7 years now, and with this experience I still get rejected. I have been able to work with cancer patients thanks to someone who was more open-minded, who gave me the opportunity to do so, and who, unlike the vast majority of complementary and integrative therapies managers, accepts shiatsu as a therapy in the hospital.

It took me five years of applying for voluntary work – and of being rejected again and again and again – to find this person.

One of the first rejections – the third to be more precise - was when I applied to take part in a pilot project with complementary therapies for adults on dialysis. With my extensive experience giving shiatsu to children on dialysis, and mentioning the informal study I have written about above, I thought I would at least have a chance to be called for an interview. They didn't even bother to reply. When I wrote to them and asked why they had not written back, and what problem they had with shiatsu, the reply was that they didn't have any problem with particular therapies, but that they had taken people who had experience in the NHS, and I was advised to offer Swedish Massage to another hospital. Not only I am pretty sure that I was the only person applying for that post who had any kind of experience with dialysis patients, but their reply about Swedish Massage seems to contradict their statement about not paying attention to the therapies offered. So much for the attempt to present complementary therapies as evidence-based medicine, and so much for talking about patient-centred care in which patients, in most places, are denied certain therapies,

therapies that those who are not denied them love and appreciate. The reason the patients are denied shiatsu is probably because obviously, no "proper" therapist would dare utter that word in a hospital.

In one particular instance, I have been rejected by the same NHS trust four times, or seven if I include when I applied to a particular hospital within that trust which I was initially told accepted shiatsu. There is a gap of about 10 years between the first time I applied and the last one, and the third time I only applied because a colleague of mine, who was volunteering in one of their hospitals, insisted I did; I didn't want to do it because I was pretty sure what the reply was going to be. The first time I applied to this particular trust, the person I talked to said that shiatsu was very hard and painful and therefore not appropriate. When I offered to treat him personally and other members of staff to prove it was not like that, he refused. I have heard other excuses – when they bother to reply. The fourth time I applied to volunteer at that particular hospital was when I saw that one of the permanent staff was a shiatsu therapist as well as a massage therapist, and I thought it would be different. How wrong was I! The third time, my colleague, a volunteer reflexologist I was volunteering with in another hospital, who also volunteered with the trust in question, heard my story about me being rejected a few years before and insisted that "things change" and that she was sure she could talk to her manager and I would be able to volunteer.

The reply came one week later. The manager said to her: "Shiatsu is not acceptable". My colleague didn't ask why. Curiously, a few years after this occurrence, I volunteered for the trust in question giving shiatsu to the staff (they wouldn't let me get near patients), and this same man, the one who said shiatsu was not acceptable, fell asleep during my treatment.

The last time I was rejected I knew their "explanations" for not accepting shiatsu therapists as volunteers were not true.

They explained about not being able to introduce a new therapy when the whole world can see on the internet that the person who rejected me introduced a new therapy. I also happen to have participated in forums where a massage therapist, who is also a shiatsu therapist, volunteered there some time ago. They said to her that shiatsu was not acceptable because they had had a volunteer whose shiatsu was very hard and painful and so they had decided that everyone's shiatsu was hard and painful and therefore not suitable for these patients. I believe this is the real cause since I have come across the same idea several times including in another London hospital where I have – after several attempts – recently started volunteering, thank God for small mercies. During my interview, one of the women told me that on a scale of 0 to 10, the previous shiatsu she had received was so painful she would give it a 10. A few days after this interview, I was giving shiatsu to this woman when, about 15 minutes into the session, she asked if it was supposed not to hurt, because so far, it had been very nice. I replied that I hoped it didn't hurt because I believe in painless treatments.

The fact remains that the NHS Trust that has rejected me four times have allowed a shiatsu therapist whose pressure is hard and painful to volunteer and have refused someone whose pressure is soft and enjoyable to do so.

The fact also remains that they have reached a (wrong) conclusion about shiatsu being painful from *only one* therapist.

I am sure they have had massage therapists whose massage was painful too, but they haven't reached the same conclusion about massage.

But I suppose that with great ignorance comes great confidence in your own knowledge, and that people draw conclusions from just one or possibly two therapists, and to prove their point, they come up with excuses and refuse to let you even show they might be wrong, or as Adlai Stevenson put it succinctly "Ignorance is stubborn and prejudice dies hard".

In another place I was rejected twice because my massage did not use oil. I still remember the second time I applied for the position. During the interview I insisted on my interviewer sitting in a sofa rather than lying on a couch to receive shiatsu, because I had seen when entering the building that some of the patients were sitting in sofas, and I wanted to recreate as much as possible the actual conditions of work. I remember too her face during my shiatsu treatment, showing how much she was enjoying my treatment and how she was relaxing. The answer, in both cases, was that *it was not the most appropriate treatment because I didn't use oil for my massage.* One would have thought that the most important thing was how beneficial was the treatment for the patients, and how much they enjoyed it, but apparently I am wrong. What is important is whether you use oil or not.

I described some of these occurrences in a Facebook group for shiatsu practitioners, and explained that I was tired of always being the only one who applied to these kind of volunteering jobs, and the only one who asked why shiatsu is not accepted, why, as the reply often comes, "shiatsu is not suitable for patients". I wanted other shiatsu therapists to be involved in my quest to find out why. The posts in the Facebook group led to two exchanges with two very different shiatsu therapists.

A shiatsu colleague from Israel offered to help me, and got in contact with the manager for a new complementary therapies service that was being introduced in a South-East London Hospital.

I was surprised that the complementary therapies manager responded positively, saying they were looking for volunteers, so my colleague put me in contact with her.

She asked if treatments would be couch-based and said we would need to develop a policy and protocol for delivering the therapy in the cancer setting, both of which I already had experience in.

So I offered to volunteer, explained that I usually work on a couch and that I have a couple of online videos showing how I do it. I also told her of my published research paper in the field of shiatsu and cancer, and sent her my CV. She emailed saying she would get back to me. This was in mid-2019. I am still waiting for a reply, a reply from a place that offers acupuncture, massage, reflexology and reiki, but refuses point-blank to even consider shiatsu. I think one could be pardoned for thinking that they view shiatsu as something truly evil.

This same person told me more recently, when a paid job was advertised, why I could not apply for the job. She said she loved shiatsu, but that in their setting they needed a multi-modality approach to patients due to the breadth of symptoms that can be treated in diverse ways. Since I was offering more than one therapy, apparently this person believes – or pretends to believe – that shiatsu cannot treat the same symptoms as other therapies, although I find this explanation from someone who claims to love and know about shiatsu, astonishing. How she reconciles her claim to love shiatsu – and know about it – with her refusal to let me volunteer would be interesting to hear. Without said explanation, I can only say it is odd.

The other shiatsu therapist who replied on Facebook is not based in the UK, but studied shiatsu in England and posted angrily in the same group, saying that I always complained as if I was encountering more difficulties than anyone else when that was impossible and that could not be the case and that I simply liked complaining. I'll let the readers draw their own conclusions.

With all these experiences, you can probably guess that I have pondered hard and long over the question of why they wouldn't accept me.

I used to think at the beginning that it was perhaps because they thought shiatsu *has to* be given on a futon. Certainly some shiatsu therapists seem to think so.

So I changed my tactics and explained that I had a very long experience giving shiatsu on the couch and to people in their beds. It did not make any difference. I was still rejected. In one case, applying for a post that meant treating people in their homes, I was rejected with the explanation that they needed someone who could deliver treatments in people's homes. One wonders if they had read the supporting statement where I explained my experience... or if they had believed it.

At any rate, I think I have finally – after many years – understood why. They mistake deep for hard, they believe that all but the lightest of treatments are strong and painful and therefore not appropriate for cancer patients. Although as we have seen, this is certainly not the case, they – for some reason that I cannot possibly begin to fathom – also believe that in shiatsu you can't apply painless pressure or even light pressure. There is no other logical explanation for the continuous refusal of introducing a therapy that, as I have already said, is one of the best practical solutions to offer treatments to hospitalised or bedridden patients, and a very enjoyable experience for receivers whether inpatients or outpatients.

That among the permanent staff who rejected my last application to volunteer giving shiatsu to cancer patients was a shiatsu therapist who works there as a massage therapist says more – I believe – about her shiatsu than about any other aspect of the service in that particular hospital or in any other.

How and why some shiatsu therapists' pressure is painful

It is true however that some shiatsu therapists' pressure is hard and painful. There is no denying that, I have heard it a few times and experienced it myself. I once had a student who came from another school and had to teach her how to soften her pressure which was quite hard to begin with and which made it very difficult for me to relax when receiving shiatsu from her.

When I went for an interview to work for a financial company in London where they had a gym for employees only, I insisted on the manager lying down on the couch and feel my shiatsu. She immediately recoiled and told me that the previous therapist's shiatsu was very painful. However, she finally acquiesced and told me how nice my pressure was. There have been other instances where I have heard similar stories.

I have already given the example of my interview to volunteer in an orthopaedic London hospital where I am currently volunteering, where I treat many different types of conditions, and where we are conducting some research in an on-going project.

At the time of writing, I have given 41 treatments to 19 patients with diagnoses as varied as multiple sclerosis, herniated discs, osteoporosis, arthritis, Tourette syndrome, epiphyseal dysplasia, etc. Of those 41 treatments, 39 were rated as being completely painless, rated as zero pain during the treatment. Not one single treatment – not even the two which were not rated as zero pain – was rated as more painful or harder when compared to other types of massage they had previously received, and 11 of those sessions were considered much more painless than other types of massage. Only 1 person out of 19 has felt delayed onset muscle soreness (DOMS) after treatments and only after the first 2 sessions.

So far, the average improvement of their conditions after my shiatsu treatments on a 10-point scale is 3.63, comparable to or better than other therapies according to the results found in the research papers of those NHS Trusts that reject shiatsu[16]

For a treatment that is supposed to be so painful and pernicious, and which is rejected on that basis by so many knowledgeable complementary therapist managers who obviously know everything about shiatsu, I think I am not doing that badly.

It is worth noting that the summary/abstract of the research paper based on the data collected about these treatments was rejected for presentation at the Research Council for Complementary Therapy conference. One of the reasons given was that "the methodology was unclear" which it is of course. Asking people if the treatment is painful on a scale of 0 to 10, and ask them to compare it to other types of massage they have previously received is very unclear methodology. It is so unclear nobody but a rocket scientist could understand it.

Without seeing how a particular therapist works and without trying out their pressure, it is difficult to establish the exact causes and remedies of painful pressure. It is usually due to several interrelated causes, but the main reason is the incorrect use of the body.

---

[16] The main result in one of those trusts, for aromatherapy, massage, reflexology and reiki treatments on a scale of 0 to 6 was an improvement of 1.59, equivalent to 2.65 on a scale of 0 to 10. Significantly less than 3.63 for shiatsu. Charlesworth, E., Hughes, J., Plant, H. and Carballo, L., 2018. Complementary therapy for people with cancer; the patient's perspective. *European Journal of Integrative Medicine*, 17, pp.26-32.

The results in another trust meant that shiatsu did slightly better than aromatherapy and the results for shiatsu are better than those for reflexology. Dyer, J., Thomas, K., Sandsund, C. and Shaw, C., 2013. Is reflexology as effective as aromatherapy massage for symptom relief in an adult outpatient oncology population? *Complementary therapies in clinical practice*, 19(3), pp.139-146.

They do not use the relaxed weight of their body and apply pressure with their muscles, which creates tension in the arms, hands and fingers, resulting in hard and painful pressure.

Incidentally, as we saw in chapter 4, the opposite does happen too. Sometimes shiatsu therapists' pressure is too shallow, not deep enough. True, it is not painful and thus better than hard pressure, but it does not result in either such an enjoyable pressure as when it is deeper, nor in such a deep state of relaxation.

Why therapists whose pressure is so hard and painful have passed their certification, I cannot be completely certain, but I believe there are two possible explanations. Either those schools do not care about their students' quality of pressure, or, much more likely, the teachers think there is nothing you can do about it, that it is a natural thing that cannot be taught, that some students naturally have a hard pressure and others do not, so they believe there is no way to teach students how to acquire a soft, deep pressure.

My students are testament that this is not the case.

Case history: working with the no-pain principle in difficult circumstances

At the hospital, I gave several shiatsu treatments to a young Swiss woman of Portuguese origin whom I will call Maria. She was an inpatient because of her breast cancer, and suffered from pain when she moved. She had to lie on her back with a pillow under her right lower back so as not to feel pain constantly. She was very keen on receiving complementary therapies and she enjoyed my treatments a lot. I think it was the second time I saw her when I began to apply pressure on her lower back – while she was lying on her back – from her right side. From looking at her face I immediately realised that it was causing pain but she felt she shouldn't say anything. I told her to let me worry about how to deliver my treatment, and went to the left.

I worked on her lower back and provided relief this time, and a few other times, by treating both sides of her lower back, the right, which was more painful, and the left, which was not as painful, but *working only from the left side*. Yes, this is the advantage of working with something as versatile and as good as shiatsu. Working from only one side is hard on me as a therapist, and I cannot always do it, it depends on circumstances, but in spite of the difficulty, if possible, I take it as my duty to provide as much comfort and relief as possible within my capabilities.

Needless to say, she was very grateful for my work on her lower back and, incidentally, she also loved the work I did on her feet.

Two case histories: inconveniencing the patients less than other therapists

These two cases are both from experiences working in a hospital. In both cases, the patients were sometimes treated by me, and sometimes treated by other therapists. The difference is not in the effect of the therapy, they were all very good therapists. The difference is that shiatsu allows one to be more flexible in the delivery of the therapy, which occasionally means that a shiatsu treatment inconveniences patients less.

The first case is of a patient who suffered from confusion and who became agitated if his immediate environment changed too much. Because of his condition, this patient could only have his feet massaged. The advantage I had is that I am able to work on the feet for a long time without having to take off the footboard. I simply stand at the foot of the bed and apply my pressure with my arms extended. There is practically no difference of how I work on other people's feet while they are on a massage couch. Although I didn't know it at the time, taking off the footboard made him agitated, so his wife approached me one day asking me to tell everyone not to take off the footboard when treating him, something she remembered I hadn't done.

Shiatsu gave me an opportunity to work with a very vulnerable patient.

The second case was that of a woman who suffered from brain cancer, quite a few mobility problems, and who had inflatable plastic leg splints fitted on both lower legs, to stop the legs moving inwards, which they did due to hip and knee problems. The splints are not difficult to remove, but, in my opinion, for a patient that has mobility issues, the less I ask them to do the better.

When I went to treat her, she told me that if I wanted to massage her legs, the splints could be removed However, I told her to let me work my own way and not worry. I simply insert my hands wherever I can and work in those areas. I am – and was – able to apply pressure on the calf muscles, both sides of the lower legs and the feet including the soles, thus providing much-needed relief to those muscles without inconveniencing the patient in the slightest. She too felt distress when other therapists removed the footboard, because she feared she could fall.

There was no chance of her falling, but that was how she felt, she needed the protection of the safety bed rails which are on either side of the bed, and the footboard, none of which I remove or fold down when delivering my treatments.

Epilogue

All the rejections mentioned are only some of those I have encountered, I simply forget many of them, but every time I talk with someone about it, or go through my old emails, I remember or see others I had long forgotten about. In spite of this, let me finish on an optimistic note.

Let me finish with two more anecdotes and an apology. First, let me say that in spite of all these rejections, I am still optimistic about what I do and the future of shiatsu. Every cloud has a silver lining. All those rejections have taught me a lot. It has taught me about the preconceptions and prejudices many practitioners in the field of complementary therapies have concerning shiatsu. The rejections have made me aspire and strive to become a better therapist, and it also led me to do research. It is quite unlikely that I would have been so involved in research if I hadn't suffered so many rejections. It has taught me to fine tune my shiatsu in the most challenging situations. But above all, it has taught me to appreciate what I do, to see that even if it is in a small measure, I can help people. In that sense, all the volunteering and work done in hospitals has brought me enormous satisfaction.

And it is high time I apologised.

Recently, I was working through an external agency at one of the hospitals that have rejected me several times in the past, giving 10-minute "massage" to the staff. I was with another therapist who does massage while I do shiatsu. We were working in the same small room with people sitting in normal chairs. My colleague, before starting with each new person, asked them to let him know if what he did was painful, while I didn't say anything. The only cries of pain came from some of his receivers, not a lot, but some of them. Not one single cry or complaint of pain, or any mention of needing less pressure came from any of mine.

And yet, he can apply and get those jobs in hospitals because he does massage while what I do is deemed inappropriate.

So I need to apologise. I apologise to all those complementary and integrative therapists in charge of running the departments and the services in hospitals and hospices. I apologise to the managers who run the complementary therapies services. They have had to suffer the affront and outrage of seeing my applications for paid and unpaid work when using that dirty word: shiatsu. It must have been truly shocking since, when they rejected those applications, they were, clearly, only thinking of the patients' wellbeing.

Just a few weeks ago, I was walking down the corridor of the hospital where I work, when a young patient who had been operated of a brain tumour came out of her room in a wheelchair pushed by her mother. They were going out to get a bit of fresh air. As soon as she saw me, she told her mother to go back to the room because she didn't want to miss my treatment which was delivered in the wheelchair. After I finished, she told me the ache in her legs had gone and that she was feeling, as always after my treatments, very, very relaxed and content.

That is my reward,
the greatest reward I could possibly obtain

REFERENCES & BIBLIOGRAPHY

Published research papers by the author

Basic explanation of shiatsu
Cabo, F., Baskwill, A., Aguaristi, I., Christophe-Tchakaloff, S. and Guichard, J.P., 2018. Shiatsu and acupressure: Two different and distinct techniques. *International journal of therapeutic massage & bodywork*, 11(2), p.4.

Shiatsu and cancer
Browne, N., Bush, P. and Cabo, F., 2018. *Relieving pressure–An evaluation of Shiatsu treatments for cancer & palliative care patients in an NHS setting.* European Journal of Integrative Medicine, 21, pp.27-33.

Differences between shiatsu and other types of Asian bodywork (with correction)
Cabo, F. and Aguaristi, I., 2020. Similarities and differences in East Asian massage and bodywork therapies: a critical review. *OBM Integrative and Complementary Medicine*, 5(1), pp.1-17.
Correction: Cabo F, et al. Similarities and Differences in East Asian Massage and Bodywork Therapies: A Critical Review. *OBM Integrative and Complementary Medicine* 2020; 5: 17

Tool to measure effects of complementary therapies
Cabo, F. and Browne, N., 2023. The Development, Validity, and Responsiveness of a Patient-Centred Outcome Measurement Tool for Evaluating Integrative Medicine Interventions. *International Journal of Therapeutic Massage & Bodywork*, 16(3), p.20.

Research projects by the author

Heisei Shiatsu as an adjunct to the pharmacological management of cancer pain.

Shiatsu: the proscribed therapy. Misconceptions and prejudice in the NHS, a narrative inquiry.

Some differences between shiatsu as practised in Japan and in Europe

Adams, G., 2002. Shiatsu in Britain and Japan: personhood, holism and embodied aesthetics. *Anthropology & Medicine*, 9(3), pp.245-265.

Acupressure studies where pressure is measured with a weight scale

Chen, M.L., Lin, L.C., Wu, S.C. and Lin, J.G., 1999. The effectiveness of acupressure in improving the quality of sleep of institutionalized residents. *Journals of Gerontology Series A: Biomedical Sciences and Medical Sciences*, 54(8), pp.M389-M394.

Reza, H., Kian, N., Pouresmail, Z., Masood, K., Bagher, M.S.S. and Cheraghi, M.A., 2010. The effect of acupressure on quality of sleep in Iranian elderly nursing home residents.
Complementary therapies in clinical practice, 16(2),   pp.81-85.

Lee, M.K., Chang, S.B. and Kang, D.H., 2004. Effects of SP6 acupressure on labor pain and length of delivery time in women during labor. *Journal of Alternative & Complementary Medicine*, 10(6), pp.959-965.

Massage studies where pressure is measured with a force sensor validated with a weight scale

Chen, P.C., Wei, L., Huang, C.Y., Chang, F.H. and Lin, Y.N., 2022. The Effect of Massage Force on Relieving
Nonspecific Low Back Pain: A Randomized Controlled Trial. *International Journal of Environmental Research and Public Health*, 19(20), p.13191.

Websites and videos where trigger point therapy, ischaemic compression and acupressure are equated to shiatsu just because most of the points coincide

http://www.shiatsu-therapy-plus.com/ShiatsuWithTriggerPointTherapy.html

https://www.youtube.com/watch?v=MK1ISOsWPjM

https://www.drgraeme.com/articles/2022/04/what-is-the-difference-between-trigger-points-acupressure-points-and-other-pressure-points#:~:text=In%20the%20case%20of%20acupuncture,explaine d%20using%20modern%20scientific%20knowledge.

https://www.realbodywork.com/articles/massage-techniques/

Research papers and books where they equate ischaemic compression to shiatsu pressure and other techniques such as Tui Na or acupressure without any regard for the quality of pressure

Trock, D.H. and Chamberlain, F., 2007. *Healing Fibromyalgia: The Three-step Solution*. Wiley.

Chandola, H.C. and Chakraborty, A., 2009. Fibromyalgia and myofascial pain syndrome-a dilemma. *Indian journal of anaesthesia*, 53(5), p.575.

Differences between shiatsu and acupressure

https://vimeo.com/user45353252

Some well-known styles of shiatsu

Namikoshi Shiatsu. Namikoshi Shiatsu does not use the concept of meridians or points from Traditional Chinese Medicine.

Namikoshi, T., 1981. *The complete book of Shiatsu therapy*. Japan Publications.

Masunaga Shiatsu. In Masunaga Shiatsu the concept of meridians originally from Traditional Chinese Medicine is important. This type of shiatsu is called in Japan Keiraku Shiatsu. Written in Japanese 経絡指圧 (けいらくしあつ), keiraku means meridian. In the West, this type of shiatsu is better known as Zen Shiatsu.

Rappenecker, W. and Kockrick, M., 2009. *Atlas of Shiatsu: The Meridians of Zen Shiatsu*. Elsevier Health Sciences.

Lundberg, P., 2009. *The Book of Shiatsu: Vitality & Health Through the Art of Touch*. Simon and Schuster.

Stress and the body

Russell, G. and Lightman, S., 2019. *The human stress response*. Nature reviews endocrinology, 15(9), pp.525-534.

Deep, slow, painless abdominal (hara) shiatsu

https://vimeo.com/312534851

Effects of shiatsu on pelvic tilt

指圧研究会論文集 II 1998-2012,　日本指圧専門学校

Sanri points

Mestler, G.E., 1954. A Galaxy of Old Japanese Medical Books with Miscellaneous Notes on Early Medicine in Japan Part I. Medical History and Biography. General Works. Anatomy. Physiology and Pharmacology. *Bulletin   of the Medical Library Association*, 42(3), p.287.

Mestler, G.E., 1954. A Galaxy of Old Japanese Medical Books with Miscellaneous Notes on Early Medicine in Japan Part II. Acupuncture and   Moxibustion. Bathing, Balneotherapy and Massage. Nursing, Pediatrics and Hygiene. Obstetrics and Gynecology. *Bulletin of the Medical Library Association*, 42(4), p.468.

Shiatsu Treatment for back pain

https://vimeo.com/144423939

Essays on meta-ignorance (or ignorance of ignorance)

Dunning, D., 2011. *The Dunning–Kruger effect: On being ignorant of one's own ignorance.* Advances in experimental social psychology (Vol. 44, pp. 247-296). Academic Press.

Stampley, H., 2020. *The Arrogance of Ignorance: What do you know?* Interface Entertainment, LLC.

Shoshin, beginner's mind

Suzuki, S., 2020. *Zen mind, beginner's mind*. Shambhala Publications.

Index

Apologies, **144–45**
beginner's mind, 92
blood clot, 50, 86
blood pressure, 96, 97, 103, 131
Brittle bone disease. *See Osteogenesis Imperfecta*
Complementary therapies lead. *See* Complementary therapies
  manager
Complementary therapies service
  managers, 129, 132, 133, 135, 139
Delayed onset muscle soreness (DOMS), 138
gravity, 76, 120, 121
ignorance
  ignorance begets confidence, 134
intention, 31, 37, 76, 88
Masunaga, Shitsuzo, 24, 26, 125
Namikoshi, Tokujiro, 24, 26, 42
NHS Trust, 17, 134, 139
No-pain principle, 24, 86, 87, 91, 93, 103, 114, 115, 140, *See also*
  painless pressure
Osteogenesis Imperfecta, 126
pressure
  characteristics, 38, 51, 80
  deep, 13, 15, 16, 28, 29, 32, 34, 37, 52, 60, 74, 86, 98, 102, 104,
    120, 137, 140
  deep and soft, 13, 28, 34
  intensity, 30, 44, 52, 74, 75, 81, 87, 88, 89
  painful, 15, 31, 36, 52, 87, 90, 98, 139
  painless, 16, 29, 30, 48, 53, 59, 84, 92, 98, 121, 134, 137, 138
  quality, 15, 16, 17, 26, 27, 28, 36, 56, 73, 140
  soft, 13, 23, 33, 140
Quality
  pressure. *See* under pressure: quality
  quest, **70–72**
Research, 21, 30, 31, 59, 124, 138, 144
  conference, 139
  paper, 21, 27, 55, 57, 80, 136, 139
  project, 24, 127
  Research Council for Complementary Medicine, 139
rhythm, 32, 76, **80–84**, 93, 100, 103, 104

Sanri points, 107
Science
  attitudes, **63–68**
Shiatsu
  abdominal, 50, 74, 84, **102–6**, 108
  cancer, 11, 122, 125, 132, 136, 137
  definition, 21, 22
  massage table, 118
  myths, 29, 125
  osteoporosis, 86, 126
  perpendicularity, 38, 51
  rejected, 17, 122, **129–36**, 137, 144, 145
  relaxation response, **96–97**
  styles, **24–25**
  wheelchair, 46, 120, 122
speed, 32, 52, 80, 99, 103, 104
  entering and exiting, 81, 82, 91
Touch
  touch and science, **68–70**
vagus nerve
  digestion, 106
Zen mind. *See* Beginner's mind

Printed in Great Britain
by Amazon

28740689R00086